Jörg Molt

The BitCoin generation

How computer nerds made the world a better place

How the Blockchain and BitCoins
changed the world and how it happened

union
DESIGN
group eG
publishing

Jörg Molt

The BitCoin generation

How computer nerds made the world a better place

*How the Blockchain and BitCoins
changed the world and how it happened*

Editor: igenos e.V.

Published by: union design group publishing, Bullay/Germany
ISBN 978-3-947355-98-3

www.u-d-g.de
Cover design by Friederike Cañadas

Table of Contents

Table of Contents

2030

A better world

It's the year 2030 and now I'm sitting here in the living room watching my vacuum cleaner communicating with the house dust mite, thanks to Blockchain and Smart Contract, whereupon it voluntarily hopped into the receptacle without much protest. Considering it was 2008, when it all started, we were the dust mites and were sucked up by the huge, ultra-fast, high-suction universe, the dust sucker, and everything we knew before was radically changed... into a better world?

My dog is connected by his collar to the Blockchain, which makes him return because the chip under his coat triggers a muscle reaction that forces him into a certain direction. The data he receives are by Smart Contract, which is coupled with my navigation, the content is imported via Cryptlets. Going for a walk with your dog in cold or rainy weather? It is all water under the bridge now.

Oh, and my neighbour married a completely unknown person on the Internet yesterday, the marriage contract and the civil registry entry was made via Blockchain. All documents such as birth certificates etc. were gathered by Smart Contract and processed to Blockchain. Now all he has to do is, wait for the good girl to be released from prison.

Elections are now voted on by mobile phones and I can enjoy the sunshine of Majorca with my nose in the sangria bowl, cast my vote without slurring by pressing a button just before voting closes.

This has led to a huge voting turnout and made projections on television completely needless as the results are evaluated in real time. In the previous election this situation caused politicians stress levels to soar. A group of seniors had started a campaign based on the motto "vote at the end".

Interestingly, this initiative generated two million followers on Facebook and was even present in the media. In fact, one minute before the closing of the poll, in the so calling polling stations, over 12 million people voted, causing a landslide for the local parties.

Our cars are now driverless taxis. The ministry of transport has decided that within cities, the computer will automatically take control over the steering of the cars. I can always order my car where I need it by satellite and Smart Contract right now. It will drive me to my specified place. Meanwhile, my buddy can make a request and my car will automatically pick him up if I approve.

Since then, we have no more traffic fatalities in the city. The thrill of driving comes only when we drive outside of the cities. I can still race with 200 mph over the motorway but at a certain traffic density my car takes over the control and I cannot influence it.

Our world has become much safer. My car has a sensor that automatically detects if I've had alcohol at a rest stop. After that I cannot drive myself.

Contracts now are legally binding done by the Blockchain, and payment is made via BitCoins. The Smart Contract blocks the sum in advance and transfers automatically.

8

If I pay instalments and one of the parties fails to deliver, the Smart Contract can take countermeasures via the ever-present Internet of Things (IoT).

I cannot start my car, I cannot get into my flat, the newly purchased TV refuses to work, the washing machine on tick is no longer pumping etc.

But also vice versa. The car salesman, who did not want to take over the warranty, had to watch as another car was automatically exchanged for mine.

The landlord, who did not want to fix the broken toilet and the dripping water pipeline, now has less money in his account because the Smart Contract has booked the installer and has immediately deducted the money from his account.

Our world has improved as we do have more justice. And most of all, the Blockchain is a time lock. How could the conspiracy theorists be that wrong!

When our past history is behind us and there are no more eyewitnesses from that time left, then you can virtually make the facts disappear. Post-factual has become the term for our society.

An event of historical significance is recorded in the Blockchain today. Manipulation is no longer possible after that. The events are stored in the Public Ledger of the Blockchain for eternity, and today it is no longer possible for anybody to twist the past and come up with absurd theories.

The banking world has said goodbye. Today nobody can really believe that there were once central agencies that managed our money and robbed us on the grounds of greed for profit, through miss-speculation and political rescue measures.

Banks have no access to accounts today they only manage the accounts. Investment advice, pension plans, etc. are only services without accounts. People have wallets, and Smart Contracts regulate the payment of contracts that are also in the Blockchain and are subject to fixed specifications. The bank advisor can only use a template to determine the general conditions.

Credit continues to be granted, even from banks. These are earmarked and a Smart Contract controls the implementation. The Blockchain is controlling transfer of ownership, rights of use and securities trading.

The bank as such serves only as an intermediary and no longer supervises the customer's money. Nowadays we do that easily on our mobile phones.

The apps are so simple that pensioners have special designed devices with two buttons:

PAY and **RECEIVE**

So Grandma goes to checkout, presses pay and is done. The cashier only scans the goods and should prevent theft.

Some supermarkets are fully automated. There are only shelf packers. The system records the shopping basket on the basis of the removed food, utensils, etc. and compares the stock with the inlaid quantity in the shopping kart. The Blockchain verifies this and sends the cashier the billing amount. Apple has a system in its iPhones, which then pays the bill in passing by, without having to keep the QR code in front of the cash register. Electronic body scanners are there to prevent theft.

Since we no longer have to put the goods on a band, we can go directly to the car and unload. No more queues in the supermarket.

Our healthcare has improved. We used to have to wait for treatment at a health resort. Documents were lost; laws were not implemented due to austerity measures, etc. Humans were divided into classes. While older people received all treatments and new methods, as guinea pigs, younger people did not receive this access. With the Blockchain it all is different. The health card is now digital in the Blockchain. I have to release it for doctors and decide for myself who sees what. Furthermore, my health records are also attached.

I no longer need a referral and can also buy medicines without a prescription, as the doctor gives his clearance to the pharmacy digitally.

Pharmaceutical companies can no longer influence which manufacturer gives out the medicine.

The Smart Contract analysis the active substance and starts a comparison across all pharmacies, which manufacturer has the cheapest product with the same active ingredient to offer.

The Blockchain has not only given us free choice, but it is lowering prices and increasing the value of BitCoin permanently.

We can buy more today with BitCoins than with the old currency. Inflation will be adjusted every 4 years, halving the production of BitCoins. The total amount of all BitCoins is limited to 21 million, resulting in a steady increase in value.

We are definitely living in a better world than 15 years ago. I still remember well how the governments and banks used to complain when big trouble hit them.
"All tax evaders, money launderers and terrorist's and what is now?" We have an adequate tax system with a basic tax and people have a basic income to which they can earn on top, for example in the service sector. Due to the higher leisure time and more holidays per year, with the same earnings, the prosperity here is much higher than ever imagined.

Due to the Public Ledger, that is the publicly accessible cash account book, there is no more corruption in politics with taxpayer's money. Everything is traceable. In the beginning, the politicians tried to deceit, but in the meantime big companies, also law firms, take care of the monitoring of state's expenditure.

Democracy takes place by referendum in the Blockchain today. The state as such is therefore only one administrative unit, which defines and monitors the purpose of the revenue, which watches over the smooth run of processing. There are still parties, but ultimately it's just about how much money is spent on which areas.

12

The once powerful weapon industry is only allowed to produce arms for securing its own country. We managed to break up the redistribution system. Also the pension fund is no longer there, because our basic income also protects retirees and is supplemented by the additional services from service sectors. We have virtually no increase in prices and raw materials such as oil, etc. are no longer important, since the electrification of vehicles that are controlled by the Blockchain and GPS accounts for almost 80 percent.

There are now 100 million computers worldwide, which run the BitCoin Blockchain securing a fast and stable network. After an increase in fees for transactions, upper limits have been set now, which cannot be exceeded. So the access remains free and even low-income earners who only receive a basic income have access.

The Internet is currently being adapted for the Blockchain technology and the first sites are already online, including Facebook, which is now decentralized. The banking landscape has changed enormously; there are no more branches. To achieve transparency, banks are now being visited via virtual reality. Hololens from Microsoft has made an international breakthrough, and we can arrange a digital meeting with the bank consultant in the living room.

He is now a consultant for capital security in BitCoin and can grant BitCoin loans. At the moment, the interest rates are paid by the increase in value of the Bitcoin and so the loans are granted. The traditional banking business does not exist anymore. The government printing office has been dissolved and central banks are a symbol of the old world that no longer exists today.

Notaries today confirm the correctness of the programmed Smart Contracts in contracting and lawyers the implementing of automated legislation. Logically, judges are also there, because machines cannot make judgements.

Our world has now given way to a DAO. That means Decentralized Anonymous Organization. When it comes to money transactions and certificates, there are no longer important departments and agencies with people in offices. The Blockchain does this completely with Smart Contracts. There are only consultants who work part-time, for example, to give information and advice on the applicable laws.

The postal service has changed fundamentally. There are no more stamps. Letters are being read by Crypto key and I can follow the letter on the Blockchain. Therefore, the classic services, such as registered mail with acknowledgment of receipt, are also eliminated.

You know, looking back when I founded the first school for Blockchain and BitCoins, I did not know what was coming and how it was supposed to come about. We were revolutionaries and many of my friends thought that eventually I would simply be locked away and the media would report that I was secretly tinkering in the basement to make a bomb that would kill humanity.

That too has changed. Media events, anything worth mentioning for posterity, are posted in the Blockchain and published there in the Public Ledger. The Public Site reports on such events daily, like a newspaper, and maintains directories about all the associated transaction numbers.

Every fart at the Vienna Opera Ball is now recorded and every embarrassment. We have Blockchain browsers, like the Satoshi Explorer. The Blockchain is so strong today and the storage capacity is so big that we now have the Internet in the Blockchain.

Man, that was a drama. When the first decentralized Blockchain browser came in and ICANN warned for the end of the information society. But who remembers ICANN today? These were once the guardians of the Internet, which guarded the keys to the key computers of the Internet. Well, the Internet can be switched off. Nobody knew that. Today the Internet is in the Blockchain. Nobody needs "guardians of the internet" anymore, as the time-magazine focus once reported.

We no longer have dog shit in our world because the DNA of a dog and the owner are recorded using the English example in a Blockchain database.

Above all, we have become a safer society. Because people store their private mail, i.e. their access to their online account, only in the Blockchain, there are no more raids and burglaries. Initially, people were robbed and forced to unlock the wallet and transfer the money through the computer. Occasionally, people's fingers were cut off to get access to the Mobile Phone Wallet. At least not having their fingers washed down the loo afterwards....

It's different today. We learned from this, and there is so-called "Banking As A Service." If you have a lot of Bit-Coins and you do not want to be a victim, you can put your BitCoins in a kind of bank. You have no online access from home anymore, just a few BitCoins, which are stored in a wallet, to go shopping etc.

If you want your 1 000 BitCoins, which are now worth 200 000 Euros per piece (yes, then, the old currency, which today only exists in history books), you must be in a room that is video-monitored, bullet-proof from the outside and one authentication only approved by a living and unharmed person. This room is scanned. You can only enter individually. The area is a high security wing. The effectuation is completely decentralised managed by Smart Contracts.

After the identification of the person is ensured, he goes into another room, drives down with an elevator and transfers it to his wallets. He does not leave the building by the entrance, but has the opportunity to use several exits. Furthermore, if he has been forced, the police from there can also pick him up. We now have wallets connected to a camera, scanning the environment for transfers, and recording sounds. So if the person is not alone in the workroom and is making the transfer, an alarm is silently triggered and the police secretly surround the house and arrest the blackmailer on the spot. Accordingly, if the criminal is waiting in front of the workroom, he can trigger an alarm through his facial expression only.

The world has become safer trough driverless vehicles; trough safety technology that is not centrally controlled and trough people's awareness that they can protect their values and can monitor the government.

We have minimum wage and a flat tax. Machines work for us today and pay the salaries. The service sector has become an oasis of well-being. Applications will be processed electronically; if you need to identify yourself on the spot at the office, the waiting areas are equipped with deckchairs and free non-alcoholic drinks. Computer voices, like the navigation one, guide you through the processes. But there are still contact persons for older people; these are people who want to earn a bit on top of their basic wage.

We live in a world where, the one who helps others in the garden for money is no longer considered a tax evader. Our economy is thriving. Teachers earn what they deserve again. Students learn with completely different methods today. The jobs of the future are digital controllers, programmers, consultants and also craftsmen, farmers, TV and radio jobs, doctors, police, kindergarten staff, psychologists, speakers, and everything else that is out there. There is no longer any insurance advisor, no classic banker, no intermediary for services or other performances. Many jobs have been dropped.

Not wrong though. The cocky investment broker next door is now working as a gardener for me :) And when I think of all the fake product network marketing in the earlier years, and those idiots who used to take money out of the pockets from people with crypto currency promises just to get a few Euros commission. They are all gone now. Today, there is no such thing, because all types of work that are offered are created in the Blockchain and are recorded for eternity. The Smart Contracts platforms, which everyone has to use, will then check for plausibility.

Today, there are only violent criminals in prisons. The world has changed. Our nuclear weapons are secured via a decentralized Blockchain. And that's why nuclear disarmament has begun all over the world as they have de facto become unusable. Our computers monitor the so-called "danger", such as North Korea, etc. A rocket launch would be destroyed during the ignition phase by sophisticated laser technology from decentralized defence satellites. North Korea would nearly have destroyed itself.

The refugee crisis of the 2010s does not exist anymore. In 2025, the Digital Human Right Pack determined that all people would receive a World Citizen ID and have the number in their skin. The database is stored in the decentralized BitCoin Blockchain and cannot be manipulated. All borders have digital scanners that capture the traveller while passing. So everyone can live anywhere.

Surely there are some bomb makers who want to destroy the system, but the World ID can track down suspects easily. We have security agencies for that. They cannot act arbitrarily, because they have to make a request to trigger off the surveillance. This is then made public and everyone, including the person who is being supervised, then knows that he is monitored and for what reason. Today, all cameras are connected to the decentralized Blockchain, so that private surveillance by authorities will become a criminal offense.

Some so clever people are now sitting in a place that dates from the 1970s. All day hippie music, no phone, no cell phone, no computer. Tree houses in front of the door, a small forest and nothing else. Living a life, in a time that no longer exists. Works wonders.

2008

The end of the free world.

I ponder

It was the year 2008. A witty year for those who believed the real estate market was a safe investment and the Lehmann Brothers a nice club protecting gay rights. Yes, we now have same-sex marriages and much more, and man has become more open-minded not to suppress our unique diversity, but to accept it.

The banks in America were special favourites of the speculators who had gambled away and now had just bonds with high risk left. Due to the interest rate that went to zero in the US for a home purchase, the buying boom began.

Your house is too small; you can buy something bigger because of the interest rates? Voilá, here it is. We simply sell the old house for $ 200 000 more, it doesn't cost anything and somebody always wants to get something bigger, then we also put in the junk stocks that did not bring us anything and give the buyer the feeling that these parcel of shares will pay for their property soon.

And so the game went on. A simple stripper owns suddenly three flats and with so many bonds and sales in a week, it didn't matter whether or not the instalments are paid at all, there is always someone who can pay for it. There is enough money.

Yes... And what really happened?

The numbers person

Maurice was sitting in his office at his Investment Company and Hedge Funds. His investors had been spoiled for months, with still higher returns, and there seemed to be no end to it. The golden egg, the jack-of-all-trades, was found and produced the American upswing. He had never seen his main investor indulge in such contentment for so long. For a moment, he wondered if it was because he was able to feed his luxury cat named Mrs Wife and this one went to bed with him again. Money is the best medicine for bored domestic cats.

But something made him uneasy. When was the last time we had seen such a long hype. And above all, what happens when everything explodes?

Ahead of him were mountains of numbers. He could have filled books with it. His restless activity was fuelled by his special ability to recognize curves from numbers and generate a risk factor.

That's how he became successful. He had always repelled his investments on time, or dismantled and resold companies after he had reached the zenith and before there was a growth stop.

Somehow everything was different here. The banking world no longer played the game. The bankers were facing higher commissions all the time and America's home builders were in a gold rush.

The seduction by 'safe money' was followed with daring investment forms. Bearer bonds were bought and sold in

20

addition to the worthless shares. It seemed as if the ailing system had healed itself and the incantations of a generation of penny-pinchers were wiped out.

He studied the columns of numbers in front of him. Again and again he looked for comparisons, underlined something here something there, and his head began to work like an immense calculator, which could blow up at any moment.

"Yes?" It sounded somewhat surprised on the phone. No wonder. It was 3 o'clock in the morning and Frank was lying next to his wife who was decorated with a cucumber mask on her face. Sex was out of the question after the surplus of sparkling wine they had that evening at the Bankers night. What kind of person goes to bed with a cucumber mask at 3 AM and who the hell calls at this time?

"It's me Maurice. And what I'm going to tell you now, you should heed. I wouldn't bet on real estate anymore. The curtain is down. The bubble is going to burst. The house is full. The canal is blocked. Your arse is on the ground ... "-" Maurice, you son of a bitch! What the hell is wrong with you? We continue as before. You should go to sleep, and then you will get a clear head again. Do you know what time it is? Take care of Alice again. So, good night! Frank slammed the phone down. He was angry. What did this college boy think about messing up his night and what did he mean by the "canal is full"? Does he want to resign? He of all people. No. That was as sure as the Amen in the church.

A decision maker named Frank

Frank had first seen Maurice 10 years ago at Stanford University. He was looking for a mathematic, analytical talent and the university had an excellent reputation for basic research.

Actually, he wanted to talk to Prof. Dr. Hattenfield. He hoped he would give him a recommendation. They knew each other from a larger stock market project and they founded afterwards Frank, Maurice & Justin's Funds, one of the largest hedge funds to this day.

Their specialty was the splitting of companies with insufficient capital and then later selling highly endowed the best parts.

On that sunny morning in August 1998, Frank did not get far. On the lawn in front of the campus entrance he spotted a boy, who ran dreamily with a pencil and painted figures in the air. He could hear this boy muttering mathematical formulas to himself. Again and again the boy ran the same route to the stone lions that formed a gate to the pond beyond and from there in a semicircle back to the starting point, right there, where Frank was.

He watched him with interest. At the same time he had to think a bit of "Rain Man", this isolated autistic person, who gained world fame through Dustin Hoffmann in the lead role.

After a while Frank spoke to him: "Hey, do you think, if we go to the cafeteria and drink Coke, that you can count better in this heat? I have a task that I cannot solve;

maybe you would like to help me, before I get in touch with Prof. Dr. Hattenfield."

For a while, this boy with the blond long hair and freckles stood frozen in front of him.

"Glad Mister, uh ...." - "Frank Cooper" - "Ah, I'm Maurice Seinfield. I love difficult tasks."

They went up the mighty steps to the entrance and through the double glass doors. The old walls were imposing with the huge halls and ceiling heights, Frank had never understood how one could spoil such old walls with these new glass doors and window fronts. The library was an abomination to him. Old beech wood is surrounded by neon-style pop culture and a huge window front. You did not need lights, even at night, because the moon seemed to crawl into the hall, it was just that big. Frank reminisced. At night, under a dim floor lamp in the library, books everywhere and me associating every creak heard with the spirits of former students. Now computers were buzzing here, it was as bright as day, and any old romanticism was lost in the cool practicality of modern times.

They went to the cafeteria, which was completely renovated a few years ago and now looked like a fast food restaurant. Aluminium chairs, the walls decorated with works by Warhol and one would think that Hundertwasser had decorated the rest. Good that there was no rolled turf here. He took 2 Cokes out of the fridge, asked Maurice if he wanted to eat something, but he declined with; no thanks.

They sat down. Considering that Frank was still slim at

the time, today you could see how his wealth has affected him.

"So Maurice, I have some calculations in my briefcase..."

He pulled out a stack of papers and Maurice realized that it seemed to be stock market prices, something he had seen from his dad, who had always presented himself as a „paper trader" until Maurice understood what a currency trader is.

"I want you to look at the numbers in the different categories and tell me what you recognise in them." The boy looked at each page for exactly 1.5 seconds and put the pages very quickly aside. Then he grinned at Frank and said, "Mr., you bet on the wrong horse." The Waterhouse stocks have had a bull run and are now entering a triangular period with downward trend. I think you have burned a lot of coal in the last few days. Sell, before it is too late.

Frank stared at him with his mouth open and was about to say that he thought it was preparing for the next run, but due to the speed and the precise answer, he could not think of anything.

To his disappointment Frank waited and burned a lot more money. This conversation would haunt him for the rest of his life.

Two hours later he finally sat down with Prof. Dr. Thomas Hattenfield. Before the greeting was finished he interrupted him. "Thomas, what about Maurice? Maurice Seinfeld."

"Oh Frank, long story. His parents abandoned the boy and our university, with reference to Maurice, received a considerable sum for his education. Until today it could not be clarified where the boy really came from. He had nothing but his name. Ronda and I took care of him. The doctor who was examining him then diagnosed a mild Asperger's syndrome. He's brilliant at maths. He works with us on the Quantum Physics team, but he'll be finished in half a year, and it's incredibly hard to recommend him because he keeps falling into his own world. He needs something where he could evaluate numbers all day long. That seems to be fun for him. He's unbelievably quick."

Bingo. That's it. Frank had the solution for his investment company. A genius with numbers that recognizes trends and can forecast accordingly. He made an offer to Maurice. However, Maurice did not want to leave his usual environment and so it happened that Frank moved to an office near Maurice's residence and the campus.

Henceforth, Maurice sat there and studied all sorts of stock market prices, bonds, company valuations and calculated possible purchase offers. These were so intriguing and meaningful that Frank built an empire together with his business partners and the house bank in the following years.

Goldman Sachs, Pricewater & Cooper looked ridiculous compared with the exact analysts of Frank, Maurice & Justin's FMJ fund. Maurice was involved as a co-partner because he knew that the boy was aware what his work was worth exactly. In the beginning, it seemed that Maurice did not need sleep at all. He worked nonstop through everything that was there and newly entered. After 3 months they had to move. Maurice's office had become too small. He needed bigger tables, for ad hoc calculations, as he called it.

At the Gorman Group Bank 2002 Christmas party Maurice then met his current wife Alice. She was thrilled about his shy nature and with her blonde shoulder long hair, green eyes and slender figure; she still looks attractive even in the most boring office outfit. She has somehow a naive expression even if she was the big shot at the bank in IT Consulting. She is no less analytic than Maurice. And so they started talking and telling each other stories about numbers. Numbers and facts could then measure the couples wedding. Everything was meticulously planned and calculated to the last. Those who didn't know the two decided that the wedding was a decision based on an algorithm and therefore a necessary logical conclusion. Who would want to contradict mathematics?

At the beginning a change in awareness

Rain pelted down. Somehow the day started weird. Insight I wanted to do something, but I felt I could not. All the ideas that I had followed, and could not be achieved were gone, like the present vapour of today's e-cigarettes (who would have thought people would get addicted without ash).

I walked up and down in my small room, which was a compromise, after all the failed projects and ideas. That was a lot, but every time it brought me further if only to learn from it. The knowledge I learnt appears in a different light today. Positive.

At that time, I did not think about new projects or experiences that would be important someday. I simply wondered where my optimism was. Each loss is a challenge, every step backwards, was a step back to the crossroads, where you can take the other path that you have previously ignored.

Anything can come, I am enjoying the day. One door closes, another opens. Those were the words I kept in mind, but today it cannot motivate myself. An unfamiliar feeling, up until then I did not know that sense of stagnancy.

A sudden impulse signalled to me: "Get yourself outside, who sits inside, will not experience anything."

Yes, and then I experienced something that would keep me busy over the next few years, which fundamentally changed my way of thinking about our world.

The digital liberator, how it all began...

In the middle of nowhere on a blue planet called Earth. The whirring of the fan in the stuffy cellar made even the woodlice go crazy. The Ikea table lamp radiates a cold light, reminiscent of the old movies, where the suspect had the lamp turned onto his face, breathing in the smoke from cigarettes. "So what's the story Joe"! If Joe would not confess, the cigarette turned out on the back of his hand, would probably help a little.

Joe was born in 1972. A computer geek. Those kids who used to grow up with home computers called the C16, VC20, C64, and Amiga, the first Apple and the Sinclair ZX81. And of course the golden times of the Atari ST and the Atari Universe in general. No dreaming of hammers and drills, burning an EPROM was the highlight. These are chips on which programs were burned and which you could then easily plug in and read out. Today we are talking about the further development of flash memory in USB sticks.

Joe lived in a world similar to the Matrix. The numbers, the mathematics, the understanding that computers produce solutions to complex tasks that was his passion. Previously, he programmed in the basement with his friends and wrote demos. Small programs, that were distributed to bring out the maximum performance out of each computer to the limits, to show what how powerful they were. These were scrolls that rippled across the screen. Music with samples, that is, with language that was previously recorded as snippets or with musical instruments. The recording and incorporation of finished pieces of music, also fragments of it, called sampling.

28

In retrospect, one cannot imagine that a piece of music with sampler fragments was a great achievement. One of these pieces of music became a huge hit on the radio. The group Okay set a milestone with their song "Okay" with the help of an Atari ST computer. Chris Huelsbeck is still considered an icon of electronic music today and has written himself into computer music history with the Turrican melody on the Amiga (a simple shooting game where one controls a lone fighter in a spacesuits).

Joe was obsessed with the idea that through the Internet, there could be a community that creates value through free distribution. That offered everyone the opportunity to share information freely and effortlessly. Expressing opinions and being listened to from the masses. That was his vision long before Facebook. The Cypher Punk era. He dreamed of digital gold. A currency regardless of cash and visa accounts. A world in which one could pay invisibly and, above all, uncomplicated and without a third party being involved. Direct from person to person.

He had been programming for a long time on a file-sharing network. Now, these days, when it was cold outside, he reflected on his concept.

The power of defeat

Joe was one step ahead and caused fear and anxiety in the music world with his program Napster.

For the first time people could exchange files directly from computer to computer. A directory showed which song was on which computer. Then the computers set up a connection via the Internet. Everybody had to run special software, the Napster program.

It was the breakthrough to stop the music industry and its extortionate prices. Due to the then sluggish lines, it took an average of 6 - 20 minutes, before a piece of music found its way onto the local hard disk. But that hardly bothered anyone. The program spread like an Ebola virus. And people of all ages began to digitise their CD and record collection, at home.

So it happened that one suddenly found rarities of long forgotten times, labels which were under wraps. Was the cost of a CD at that time up to 45 Euros, tumbled the price in the following years down to 15 Euros. A paradise for music lovers and collectors. At the same time, it reduced the price of vinyl, which later in the 2000s regained its importance for the DJ scene.

The music industry was close to extinction, until it found its lifesaving change. There was an opportunity for them to turn off the computer (server "operator"), which kept lists of which computer had which piece of music. A whole series of similar programs, such as E-Donkey, could be turned off like that. The music industry filed legal action against every server operator they could find.

They were sure they had won the fight. Once and for all, having regained digital control.

Joe was celebrating the year before, before Napster went offline. He had achieved the first breakthrough. He had perfected Napster. To the extent that you can turn off the server, but that it was connected with several other servers so there was always a mirror file of the directory.

He called these junctions 'Tracker'. They also took over the task of controlling downloads from several computers that had the same file.

Joe saw himself as a knight of liberation. While Napster initially transferred the whole file, his network, which he called Torrent Net, was able to split a file, no matter what, into small packets. These were numbered. If several computers have the same files and provide them for the network, the trackers can coordinate which packet number has not yet arrived and where there is a similar sub package in the immediate vicinity. Just imagine 2 postmen who have 4 packages, belonging together. An order from Otto shipping. Four packages go to Müller street and four packages to Max street. Now Postman 1 has the parcels for the Max street and Postman 2 for the Müller street. However, because Postman 1 still has to briefly enter Weber street and Postman 2 has to go into Koch street, Postman 1 is closer to Müller street and Postman 2 is closer to Max street. Since the packages and their contents are completely identical, they can nevertheless be delivered in a very short time.

Of course, it will actually bother the customer that his name was not on it, but in essence he got exactly what he wanted. A 10 Euro note with the number XYZ does not interest the receiver either. Main thing he becomes a valid 10 Euro note.

This principle has made the Torrent network extremely fast. The test environment ran perfectly. Now he just had to convince his friends and bring the program to the public.

In the beginning, it looked a bit funny, completely different than expected. Big companies like Microsoft suddenly used his program.

It was the first program of its kind that could send huge
files directly from recipient to recipient. Email programs
are limited, and uploading a file to a server and the following download took far too long. The lines had just 768
Kbytes / sec in the download and 256 Kbytes / sec in the
upload. Today we have speeds of up to 100 MB / sec and
more in the download and up to 50 MB / sec in the upload.
The Internet of the past seems like a steam locomotive
that is being overtaken by the ICE. People would get off
during the ride because they thought they were standing.

Joe poured himself a whiskey, smoked a cigarillo and created something that changed the world, completely out of
the shadows. When Napster was discontinued in 2009, its
program came to the proud honour of being today's 1/3
of all Internet traffic. And you cannot turn it off. Although
there are several servers that can be shut down, companies use the Bit Torrent network for file transfers. The
overall economic damage at shutdown would be immense.

The Nerds

The computer featured a page called "Pirate Bay," and that was not the epitome of an online game, where you build up a sea empire under the infamous flag, even though Johnny Depp has already become the epitome of a pirate like you wish to see today.

Yes, not even the site of the Pirate Party, which would later be of high importance for a short time. Until the frigate collapsed under the weight of the mutineers.

Fred Barnsley is a guy like you and I know from high school. The little fat boy, who at the All You Can Eat Day of Pizza Hut, eats everything away, and now reaches puberty with pimples all over. His appearance looking like a Marguerite with glasses. The cheese crust could be the arched protruding ears that hung down like rags on his circular face. That's why the kids called him "Fat Fred". But that did not interest him. He spent his spare time in front of the computer. Online Games, World of Warcraft, that's what the 2000s did. Dr. Kimble, also called Kim Schmitz, was his role model. This fatso had so much money that everyone who tried to sunbathe in his shadow froze to death. He was the head of digital freedom. He founded Mega upload, which allowed him to anonymously store his films and files on a server.

Fred got his software and all the movies and music from Pirate Bay and Bit Torrent network. He saved the movies and everything else at Mega upload. For eternity.

The music and film industry managed to scare off a few people. Dr. Kimble was picked up, just like in a film, from his estate in New Zealand, with a special commando, which stormed the property. However, he was not extradited to the USA. It was often a legal case study, including indentation, played up by the music industry medial, because they could prove that illegal file-sharing (the distribution of films and music) was being operated, but the technology carried on. Companies specialized in putting so-called false items into the Torrent network and pinpointing someone based on their IP address. The IP address is an invention of the Internet. Every computer connected to the Internet gets an IP address, i.e. street, house number and place of residence, so that the Internet postman knows where to deliver which parcel.

Fred had figured out how to build a VPN at a computer congress with a few other freaks. This means Virtual Private Network. So not a real existing, virtual, private network. More like an invisible Internet between different computers. Although everything is transported through the normal Internet, it succeeded to hide the address from its own computer, he simply becomes a new one. To do this, Computer A calls another Computer B, before going online, Computer B than establishes for A the Internet connection. You can choose, where this should be today, because the larger VPN operators have created a decentralized network of dial-up computers, distributed around the world, they cannot be disengaged.

If you use such a VPN, then you can use file sharing, without a warning from a lawyer. When he checks the address, he finds an address somewhere in Africa or America or elsewhere. This means that a warning is meaningless and in vain.

No, here is the digital freedom, music and film as a common resource. The freedom of digital humanity, anonymous and decentralized, to get everything for free. GEMA, record companies, film rights holders and exploiters are powerless to this day.

At times, Napster was the fastest growing Community of the Internet. This can be explained by the cost-free system and attractive content. Shortly before its demise in February 2001, the Napster community had about 80 million users worldwide, of who 1.6 million were constantly online; in January 2001 alone, the exchange volume was around two billion files.

The blind man can hear very well but runs without sound into the wall. By court order, the register to which the computer in question disclosed which other computer stored the piece of music, was closed.

With the Bit Torrent network, the industry shot itself down, without understanding why. It was too late to switch off and that's what a huge community including Fred has been enjoying since 2002. The world is beautiful. And pizza even more beautiful. Enjoying he had bite off. Years later he succumbed to his weight. But that's another story and can be told another time by someone else. The pizza, however, became a symbol of the new beginning, which was to complete redesign of the world once and for all.

A visit that changed everything

I visited my friend Jack on a cold rainy day in 2008. I've never been sure if his name was a pseudonym. I met Jack at a paintball session where we delivered a merciless battle on an old factory site. In different teams. At the subsequent barbecue we came closer and finally became friends.

Jack Gomez, as he called himself, was one of those obscure but intriguing types. He was not that nerd, spotty, with a 3-day beard and a pair of underpants pulled over his head, waiting for the end of the world. He was not one of those guys who spent their social life in role-playing games wasting away in the dark, leaving only to do a hated job. He was sporty, about 1.80 m tall, blonde, half long hair, and the typical surfer guy from Hawaii.

Jack grinned all over his face as I entered the door. We had not seen each other for some time. I was busy with my job, a boring office job in administration, since the reform I could not save myself from claimants and regularly worked overtime, while Jack was just finishing, what felt like, his sixth relationship!

The computer in his office was buzzing away, the monitor flickering and a thought arises. The drawer is opened and the notebook taken out. But where is the pen? Sure, you could put everything in the computer, but the old paper block of the offline world is still faster.

"I have to show you something; absolutely ... you have to take this out into the world ...."

Yeah, and then somehow the idea of communism suddenly shot through somebody's head (it was never implemented because one had decided to make himself rich and leave the common good to the others): If we had a world, in which there would be no centrality, it would be fairer.

It's not so that romantics did not dream of living in a decentralized world before, where a majority of the fair-minded decides what happens in the future. We have seen many grandiose projects fail because charitable work cannot be reconciled with economic principles and, if so, the good ones get themselves screwed. An airport in Germany that will probably never see any airplanes, because everyone in the money swamp is striving for the power and influence from this prestigious object. Should it be ready after years, it will already be too small. An Elbe Philharmonic (Hamburg), which is not sufficiently protected against a spring tide, and thus after years of construction and an accompanying increase in price of 500%, will cause a black hole of billions. Maybe they will play the Titanic theme in such a case.

Globalization has moved a great deal and the voices of those who equate it with the loss of independence and freedom have been rejected as innovation barriers.

A few people are directing the world today and the population are treated like side effects, as the fans in a football stadium, if one sits in the VIP lounge.

The main problem is that people have lost their self-determination and control over their assets.

Banks and government can block accounts, track any movement, and almost anyone today can be fully monitored through social media. The world population has accepted promises that were nothing but Valium being thrown into a piranha basin. Saturated fish do not bite. Governments have introduced ever more absurd tax inventions, in order for the state to have zero new debt, and more and more people are living in poverty.

And then, as if coming from a foreign world, a Mr. Snowden came, who had not yet known that his "adopted residence" would be Russia.

An outcry went around the world and for a moment even the normal mortal realized that there is no such thing as privacy.

At the end of 2008, however, something had happened which, 7 years later, terrified the elite of the world and calmed the citizens.

Except for a couple of geeks with computers, no one had learned that the solution would be computer science and maths.

It was 8 o'clock in the morning and Maurice's decision was taken. He had counted all night and now it was clear. A clarity in the bright blue sky after a foggy night. This clarity gave way to certainty and left nothing else to do but act.

He drove to Lehmann Brothers. The bank that held the most mortgages in the area and had previously earned a fortune on the real estate boom. "Greed rots your mind". With that in mind, he entered the office of Sam Bernarson. Sam was a haggard man in his mid-thirties and a real estate investment manager. Sam had powerful decision-making powers, and he made sure that everyone in his office and in his private life knew about that. Friend were fading in to employees in his presence, he left no opportunity out to tell everyone that he had made it and People should be happy just to dine out with him or hang out in one of several clubs he visited.

Sam loved women because he could buy them. His Ferrari 420 GT helped him getting countless women in his bed and he enjoyed it. True love didn't exist for him. That was called Lehmann Brothers and he would die for it. His estimated fortune was approximately $ 8 million. A lot of bucks for a pizza maker. He did not realize that, at the time Maurice entered the office, it would soon turn in to ashes.

Maurice smiled and Sam approached him openly. "Maurice, you number nutter. What has your brain figured out again, what do you want to buy? Dismantling the North Pole and the Christmas Man Factory into a fairy elf franchise?" He smiled looking just like one of those winning smiles out of a dental advert.

Maurice smiled back briefly. Then he became serious. "Sam, it is not going to carry on like this and no Frank does not know that I'm here, he did not want to listen to me last night."

"What's not going to carry on?" His eyes searching with his eyebrows arched. So Maurice went through the numbers he had brought with him, and then there was silence for a moment. "Finally," thought Maurice, "he's got it! Thank god for that. "But the thought vanished as fast as it came. Sam's statement "I think you've got the numbers spinning around in your head like a SODOKU, you don't see the reality anymore."

A thought came in Maurice's head and he tried to use Sam's vanity "Sam, you did not just become a banker because of the numbers, but because you're in charge of a team and they all listen to you because you made the bank rich. How can it be that you are so misguided?" Indeed, that touched Sam.

"Do you doubt my astuteness Maurice? Do you not see that you are the only one who follows such a crude theory? Maurice, you're overtired, you can't even see it anymore. The real estate market is as sure as the Amen in the church, as sure as Jerry beats Tom and as sure as how Ben & Jerry make the Americans even more round!"

"Okay Sam, let's bet. Agreed?"

"What do you want to bet on, you will lose just by thinking about it? Leave it!"

"I offer you a million each month when the real estate upgrade continues. In return, I demand that in case of a crash, the creditor's compensation will be paid to me, before the rest becomes anything."

"Maurice, you've lost it! What happens to Frank and his legacy? And the best investment company of all time, you will ruin yourself and him."

"Sam, the creditor's liability is somewhere in the 3-digit millions. This will put an end to the banks 100-year old history and it will change the future."

"Maurice, I KNOW WHAT I AM DOING, I will accept the deal but don't come on all fours, like a mangy dog who has bitten his master and now begs for mercy and food, in the form of a rescue loan. Roger that?"

"Deal Sam?"

"Deal! Bob will set up the contract, he is our new house notary, and now go away before I change my mind!"

"Sam, you have made a big mistake. See you, one way or the other."

Maurice went home. "Such a pig headed fellow", were his words as he came home, with rings under his eyes, and his wife took him into her arms. Alice hadn't seen him so upset before. He was her sunshine, an analytical morning ray at dawn.

Today more like the right hand from Zeus, the lightning. Thrown out of infinite space to destroy everything. Serious thoughts went through her head but she better kept them to herself. What Maurice had told her was so hair-raising that she saw Maurice and herself moving in with her parents. Broke and burned out, looking for a meaning in life. If she would tell him that now, he would go crazy, that she was sure of.

The conversation with Frank ended in Frank looking like a walking corpse. He went to his office without saying a word and phoned wildly. Maurice knew with whom, the lawyer and notary Dr. Spenger. He was the man for all cases. He could simply dissolve contracts that were waterproof, or convince the other side to simply dissolve the contracts. An art he had mastered, like a dog, gathering the sheep together.

Once released, Spenger was unstoppable.

He dived into every deep and filthy swamp. Did not sleep for several weeks of research until he found the flaw. And then he grappled hold of it. Like a pack of hungry hyenas would do in a ravine with a lost tourist. He was ferocious, which had already made some companies lose their head; they were then mercilessly bought up by FMJ.

But in this case, nothing worked. Maurice had made the contract so waterproof and to bring down the Lehmann Brothers, was not possible because FMJ itself was involved in a holding, which was an offshoot of the bank.

Frank did not talk to Maurice anymore. He was numb to the outside world. Every month he lost a million. That was the end of the free world for Frank.

Never, but really never, would he have thought it possible that Maurice was the one, the ingenious chess player of numbers, the god of mathematics, his foster son and his best friend, who would rip him off so much. Frank was sure that he would lose everything and even his wife, who will finally see him as a failure. Just the allegations: "You always said, you're the boss, do something at last, instead of stupidly looking up in the air." And he would reply: "It cannot be done, I do not control the situation any more" and such a sentence would drive his wife crazy, she would pack her bags and drive off to her mother. And her mother was not just a dragon; it would be a combination of the worst nightmares imaginable.

The first months were so hard for our analyst Maurice that he drove around the area by himself looking at the abandoned houses that were no longer in earning status. Some stayed empty for months, the mail piling up to the ceiling. Many became homes for the homeless. Electricity and water was turned off and there was a smell of urine. Abandoned dogs strayed through deserted settlements in search of some food.

But nothing happened. Payment was made diligently every month and just before the bankruptcy it happened... the big bang, the total meltdown,... the debt wave crashed over the selling wave. The tsunami came without announcement. Within 36 hours Lehmann Brothers were bankrupt and with it many other banks. Maurice had given his company a billion-dollar gift.

The burst of the real estate bubble had produced a shock worldwide. The stock market shake up, the disaster beyond all expectations for the capitalist world. Nobody knew until now, how much Lehmann Brothers were really connected with the banks and governments of the world. In Germany, the taxpayer had to save the banks, which sits on bad loans in billions of Euros due to their involvement, and should these no longer be handled, the bank would destroy itself.

Even ten years later, Italy would not be able to get back onto its feet cowering under the huge bank sword of Damocles.

What at first seemed like a big joke left hundreds of thousands of people worldwide jobless. And someone hanged himself after the news, on a sunny Friday afternoon in the office. The colleagues were gone. He performed the last transaction of his life and transferred Maurice the creditors' compensation, knowing that this would be the end of the small investor and the average person who would be left to live on the streets.

It was the first time in the history of, the growing control mania' as Snowden described it, that the earth was woken up. Worldwide demonstrations and turmoil brought governments under pressure. It seemed for a moment that everything was about to change. But that was just a bubble on the rim of a freshly filled piccolo glass. What came later was the final battle between the state and its citizens. A fight for life and death all over the world.

The end of the financial world in 2008 became the beginning of a new epoch in human history, more signifi-
i
cant and greater than the Internet was before and could ever be. This epoch should offer people a choice. A choice of freedom that had been lost till now and many people had only one thing now: fear and anxiety. However, only those, who believed in central structures and in the restoration of the old life and in the power structure. Those politicians were the victims to a regulatory delusion. And those who believed they could re-structure the world into a world order of dictation. People who believed that free will can only be teachable if there is a central power that puts an end to the different minded and creates uniformed people.

Jack

On that day, I actually decided to stay home but then ended up in Jack's office. YES, he was right with his remarks about centrality in our world and also that, a

44

one-sided control would put us into slavery.
He scribbled with his pencil wildly on his block while trying to explain the world to me.

Jack has always been the "lightning bolt" among my friends and at school. He was able to mathematically justify circumstances very quickly resulting in dream notes in maths and physic. Sometimes, after talking to him, I thought he was from another world. He told me something about the refraction of light in the time / space, leaving no stone unturned to introduce me to the secrets of crypto-coding or his new research on peer-2-peer networks.

It was a passion I shared as little as a fish fishing with a fisher.

Jack ranted on as he wrote some formulas in the block and painted pictures. "A revolution, the power of independence, the downfall of the money-eagle, in short the entire change in our coexistence and its exploitation and its paranoia of surveillance."

Then he handed me his notes and I was waiting for his favourite saying: "Open up your mind, or you will not understand it, you dusty office amoeba."

But he did not need to say that. I understood everything at once. It was so clear to me that I was going haywire on it.

Jack had done nothing but showing a drawing that could set the scene for the end of our society, and whose discovery will bring about even more change than the Internet today.

He had created 2 things and was now about to start the computer and show me:

1. He had perfected the Bit torrent network. There are no servers or nodes in his network anymore. He managed to write the software that unites client and server in one computer, so that everyone also becomes the node who installs the software. At Bit torrent it was still the case that everyone had to install the program (client) and then control the external servers, where the files are and where they should be delivered.

2. He has created an algorithm that can safely send a payment from A to B. To do this, you convert money into so-called BitCoins. These are then sent via the client, which is called wallet (purse), through the network to the recipient client (wallet).

On the way there, at least 51 percent of the computers must verify the transactions using a mathematical / physical procedure. Then the transfer is entered in a publicly accessible directory and is valid for all time.

The trick is that this directory will be mirrored at the same time, during the preparation, on all 600,000 computers.

"Jack!!! How the hell do you manage to have 600,000 people running this software day and night, and it doesn't break down?"

"Okay, that is really easy. We started with five computers to send the BitCoins back and forth. Because somebody is doing this now, a computer in our BitCoin network will be rewarded with new BitCoins every 10 minutes, according to a random principle.“

“Come on, Jacky, they do not have any value, it's craziness, 600,000! Just think, they're doing that for some Coins that are worth nothing? Being bored brings out blunders by rich people...”

“And what if I tell you now that a pizza has been baked that was then sold for 10,000 BitCoin and that BitCoin has a commercial value? That's exactly what has happened! For a long time, I looked like I was paralysed. When 600,000 people send BitCoins back and forth, that cannot be so precarious, otherwise everyone would have jumped off already.

“What happens when the Internet dies off?” - “Around the world? Are you crazy? I think you wouldn't care what would happen to your BitCoins, and then humanity has some quite different problems” – “And when the network starts up again, is everything back?”

Jack wanted to show me something else, not that my head wasn't already dizzy. He actually showed me how a friend in Africa received BitCoins within ten minutes.

“Guess how much that costs? Nothing! Correct!“

“And no one can stop this, no government, no bank?”

“No, the Blockchain is an Internet above the Internet and thus works in a different way. Every computer, including yours, that runs the software, becomes a node at the same time. So that means, the BitCoin is only in the Blockchain, that's what I call it, and cannot be found in the Internet. Although they are all somewhere on your computer now, because of the crypto key you are not able to replace or manipulate the file. We have already tested this. The experts agree that to 99,9 percent this cannot be hacked in the next ten years."

I almost blacked out. I got something to drink and we went over to the living room, where his new flame, a black-haired, long-legged beauty, seemed to float over the carpet and serve the food.

"And what does your friend say, Jackie?" She asked lecherously.

"Well, I think he understands that we can put our money system in the bin after the total meltdown and can build a world currency with BitCoins so that there is no more corruption and trickery. And he probably also realized that this cannot be turned off by a government. As an economist, he has probably figured out that, when the BitCoin will be traded on exchanges soon, where that it is leading to."

I answered; that I felt like I had a drunk from the light of knowledge in the universe and that it was so beautiful, that I actually did not really intend to return to earth. A money system, which identifies all transactions with numbers and holds them in a public book, which can neither be forged nor exchanged, and where only numbers instead of names stand, that's a dream. Privacy, secure asset management and I do not need a bank that generates real estate bubbles and burns my hard-earned money. And best of all, it works worldwide.

48

"Listen," he said, "you have to know that I'm not the inventor of the system, but just showing you that it exists. There is a certain Satoshi Nakamoto who showed up on the Internet. Totally anonymous and he posted this and showed how it works. However, as it looked, someone in his immediate vicinity wanted to talk to the government and the CIA about it. Satoshi then went into anonymity and never showed up again, but left his gift there. The perfect algorithm!"

I had just recovered a little, now this tingling atmosphere came over me, caused by a few secret people in even more secret backrooms, where they were putting their clever heads together, hidden from the world, and nothing other in mind than to rescue people from Government power and banks.

From that day on, I was a different person and started my mission. To lead people back into their self-determination. To show people how ingenious and safe this technique is. And that they cannot be ripped off anymore. That they should set themselves free of the debts and lies in the banking system.

Jack and I sat together for a very long time and decided to start a mining farm and I thought about chickens, cows and tractors with wide fields and the cock at six o'clock in the morning that wakes us up....

The things that wake us today are the positive messages and the awareness to change the world, every day a new, always a bit more and always good.

The digital money revolution

Satoshi Nakamoto

A phenomenon, a spiritual genius, an alien sent to liberate mankind. A group of highly intelligent people who have created something unique? Is it even a movement, like the hippies or Bhagwan movement. Is this a digital sect? Can such good people actually exist, or is this a government's attempt to get us all under total surveillance?

What Satoshi Nakamoto, and I assume that he was a lone perpetrator, had made here, has definitely changed our lives in 2017.

Guys, you've been sleeping! In 2008, something began to creep in, like a newborn virus waiting to become Ebola and trigger a pandemic. A virus that meanwhile had been implanted into over 1 million heads and users voluntarily installed this virus on their computers.

Our world is no longer 1972 or the 1980s. Our world today is, as in the movie "Public Enemy No. 1" from the 1990s or as the folk hero Snowden has shown us, we are no longer free, but totally supervised. There has been no privacy since 2017.

And in the midst of plans for a new world, that the most powerful of this world are hatching, in the belief that when people are centrally governed, there is no more war, then comes the liberation of modern slaves. In the shape of a computer program. Everyone can exchange their money in BitCoins and free themselves from the local money traffic and the associated restrictions. Whether in Russia, China, Japan, Africa, Australia, Europe, one system that is the same for everyone. Free trade, absolutely safe and above all from person to person, without an intermediary.

You can just do it. Nobody can forbid it. This thought has led to millions of people setting up their computers and letting it run. The world is full of new innovations today, thanks to this technology. But where did it all start? Let's take a closer look at this on the next pages.

One virus, two sides:

The good side:

On the one hand, the sweet lure of finally bringing people together and allowing globalization as a means of payment and control through the Blockchain and not only for industrial nations, but also for the poorest of the poorest. For those who have a cell phone or have a community sharing a smart phone or a computer.

Finally, participate in the financial system of a new world in which there is no exploitation. Only benevolence. Send money to relatives without bank charges and similar charges. At least not so much!

A free world of payments.

Then came the development of Smart Contracts, which allows us to transfer the system to all sectors. We no longer need notaries, no intermediaries and can do business from person to person.

Nobody can stop the system anymore today. No regulation, no ban can shut down the system. No government can forbid it. Free access. Over 1.6 million computers scattered around the world, by the neighbours, in a server farm or on an island. Blockchain and BitCoin has become a decentralized network of businesses and individuals that cannot be shut down. Thanks to so-called paper wallets, BitCoins can be used like cash, without a computer. But we'll come to that later; otherwise your brain will be overflowing with input. What a world!

All we have to do is learn to act on our own and, above all, carefully.

The negative side:

The threat from corporate power, i.e. the financial institutions and governments, has lead to, the evaluation and trade of BitCoins as a stock market paper, ensuring that BitCoin is absurdly regulated from central authorities.

Our world today is clearly structured: America, Russia and China determine world politics. Europe cleans up the mistakes resulting from this constellation and wrong decisions, and Africa is kept as small as possible, people are not adequately educated enough, keeping the prosperity of the western world, Russia and China alive. At least in China's- and Russia's upper classes, where alongside oil and other businesses thrived at the expense of the common good, the communism lives.

In the West, all this has led to the public is being led by puppets on a string trying to get the attention of world governments.

On one thing, though, everyone agrees, superpowers or Western governments see refugees as a threat to prosperity. So these people must be excluded on the assumption that they eventually organize themselves or die. Which, cynically said, somewhat restrains the problem of over-population. Wars, where dumb people who believe in a better future die as food for sharks, which is still better than sickness and hunger.

But this presupposes that the maker of this order has the power. Power is exercised through faith and politics.

Now, the mighty have realised a bit too late that the Block-chain technology and the BitCoin is standing opposite to their ideas of it being a great risk to our present system. Interestingly, this could happen because the generation that controls the system comes from a world that has always been told, "Kid, computers are no good for you, go outside and play." Today no one needs such thinkers of yesterday. With the Blockchain technology, the nerds of former days hijacked world politics and allowed people to choose: escape to freedom or remain in the old system out of fear for self-responsibility.

The governments in fear of what might happen gave warnings out thus creating fear and mistrust, which ordinary people, who had never learned to speak up for themselves follow. "They'll know what they're doing up there."

How many times do we hear the phrase, "Let someone do it who knows what has to be done!"

Or this sentence, which on a long term has always created

fear in our subconscious mind, even though one laughs about it: "I can fix that myself, ...ooops, broken!"

The BitCoin reminds us of what we in fact want to be, self-confident human beings, who decide themselves want they want. But it also reminds us that there will be nobody to blame for our failures.

As long as there is „the ones up there", "it wasn't me, that was broken before" and passing down the blame from top to bottom in companies is common, there is not really total freedom. Freedom comes from the courage to stand up and say, "Okay guys, I was convinced that was going to work and now I've screwed it up. So can I ask you to support me and help me to fix that!"

But we will not hear this. Also not from any politician. Why? Because it is a sign of weakness.

So we will not hear from politicians: "We were sleeping when the BitCoin came, so we'll make the most of it and just accept it."

What we experience is one disaster after another. To produce BitCoins, there are so-called miners. No, mining in the Ruhr Valley is dead and will stay that way! This has something to do with the computer process, which makes sure that BitCoins cannot be faked and why there can be more BitCoins. We will discuss that later.

The people, who use their computers for this nebulous mining, have been punished in China with the dead penalty and persecuted in Russia. Ultimately, the governments have given in seeing they cannot prevent it happening.

In Venezuela, people are still being imprisoned, and Argentina is also fighting against the digitisation of money.

The good side of the virus is winning

Through such measures, governments have suffered a great loss of confidence. People in countries where national currencies are worthless, inflation barely makes it possible to buy food, it does not matter if they are imprisoned or starved to death. These people are just using it. There is no discussion. And they can see that it works. It does not matter if you have to wait 3 minutes until the money is there or 10 hours. The actual usage and getting away from being dictated too, is the best thing that can happen to them. They can afford things that were previously excluded from. And above all, they can afford EDUCATION. Now the education endangers the ignorance and people should stay ignorant.

The BitCoin does not need permission. Nobody to ask about it. Just a bit of education, how to get into the system and how to deal with the money. So exchange and transfer. Once learnt, it's like cycling. We can start cycling, but still have to pay attention so we will not get run over by a car. This means we use BitCoins, but we have to be careful that we do not get ripped off.

The world can work so easily and in many countries it already works like that. Japan, Hawaii, Philippines, Switzerland, Austria, America and more recently Africa. Many countries are opening up to the BitCoin thus becoming a sustainable economic system. Unfortunately though there are the exchange offices, which are exploiting and regu-

55

lating transfers.

The good thing, however, is that there are more and more decentralized exchanges and that people can still use the Bazooka Paper Wallet against the government and financial industry.

BitCoins can, as already mentioned, also be used as comparative cash. This knowledge is now spreading and soon it will be available worldwide. Platforms like localbitcoins. com have given a boost to decentralism.

So much for the theory, but now let's move on with Satoshi Nakamoto ... this story is fictional and free of any logic except my own, which I allow myself to present here, because I think I feel it, I can put myself in the 'world of thoughts', and that is at least for the moment very down to earth.

1995

The awakening of the Internet era.

Yes, there is an Internet and yes we have emails. George was annoyed. The "big business" promised by the consultants of Merchandise & Co failed. Nokia already has a few models that can use the Internet, but it looks like the first Casio watch. Using it with three hours waiting time, just crap.

And it does not look better at home either. We surf with a 768-kbyte-line, which the friendly voice from Telecom praised as a revolution. "Imagine surfing the Internet now is like browsing through a book." Funnily enough, 20 years later the promise was still not happening, even with 100Mbps. Although much faster, thanks to Google Chrome, but sometimes it falters and gets hung up, because pages are overloaded or the expansion with fast Internet in rural areas has never taken place.

George sat in front of his PC and surfed via AOL in the vastness of the Internet. There were not too many pages yet, Google was in its infancy and so I was still using a spider-crawler as a search engine. This technique was able to quickly capture and display many pages, but not for sophisticated search terms, only for simple word searches.

He stumbled upon an article that prophesied a free world thanks to Internet. Later, one would attribute these articles and more to the so-called Cypherpunk era.

A decentralized world, where overall information is common knowledge raising the educational level of all humanity, meaning a better, more prosperous world and also taking into account the third world.

Sounds good! George had always felt that people could only develop through open communication and free reporting.

George Burnsby was actually a head mechanic for cars and had a thriving workshop. He only worked him self privately or for friends tuning cars. His workshop employed 20 young lads who could do everything. Talented mechanics, who could even bring a rusty VW Bus back to life.

He was a dreamer; so earlier in school they always called him "spaced out". George could not get along with his fellow humans. Two failed marriages, fortunately childless, made him doubt human destiny, and the losses that his once radiant beautiful and good-natured first wife had brought him after she became a fury, that in itself made him doubt what the whole meaning of man and woman, except of course for reproduction, could be. His second wife, a math professor, was so factual that he partially believed, if she is as structured as a car, nothing could go wrong. This misbelieve did not last long either. When she started to put on weight, she said "Darling, how do you like me?" He replied, "Yes, great. Like a compact car.", which led in the subsequent debate to the separation. He was never a man of numbers and therefore she was able to pay him off and he lost his workshop, their shared house, including the dog!

But because of his incredible talent he was able to rebuild everything. Now he lives on visiting the local beach club now and then, and like he always said, "having sex without expectations" is better. He realised this after learning that taking out a woman, spending a lot of money, did not lead to the desired success or they wanted to move in with him immediately.

Nope, he does not want obligations and that's why it's good like it is now.

His computer and the Internet were his hobby to find sympathizers. Facebook was still far away for him and therefore only pin boards and a mailbox system, which acted thematically, remained.

The decentralized restructuring of humanity fascinated him. Although he had no idea how to do that, except surfing, a computer was a sealed book for him, but he had some romantic ideas and wrote a post in a forum:

In which society do we want to live?

Humanity has to organize itself, because the heads of states have lost their sense of community and are starting to use absurd methods to spy on their own citizens. They want to influence us with threats that are not there and blackmail us with our money, which the banks can withhold, at will, by public policy, by a government. Freedom stops with money regulated from central governments and starts with the liberation from central authority. WHAT DO YOU THINK?

In the coming weeks and months, a worldwide discussion

began. Participants from all over the world began to philosophise feverishly about a new decentralized world order. There were a few weirdoes, but also ones who began to develop concepts.

Somewhere in another place, another computer, another country, Satoshi sat in front of his computer. He had grown up in modest circumstances and computers were his life. Windows 95 was the evolution of the user interface and was better than the start of Geos on the C64. He used Netscape and he was impressed with the digital new world and the possibilities of the Internet. He was much further than George. He worked on his own company pages and offered services for others. He lived well, but the discussion left him no peace.

Someone had developed a concept using digital gold. A theoretical model of how the development of money can be managed only by computers. Practically speaking the computer acts like its own bank account.

The only problem is how to protect the data from theft? A network would indeed work only by connecting the computer directly. So over the Internet. So far so good, but what if the line breaks up during the transfer and the money disappears? Or someone reboots his computer, because Windows is showing a blue screen and nothing works?

That sounded all romantic, but not realistic. He reflected, at some stage he had heard somebody talk about a cryptographic encryption approach that included two key pairs, private and public. This theory dates back to 1976, when Whitfield Diffie and Martin Hellmann theoretically discussed this possibility and which was then scientifically and practically documented as the so-called RSA method from Shamir, Adlman and Riefest at MIT. This procedure didn't offer to possibility to be attacked. RSA stands for the first letters of surnames.

Already in 1970, a similar procedure was developed by the GCHQ (Government Communication Headquarter - 007 says hello!) in England, but not scientifically documented because of secrecy. In 1983, therefore, the patent was filed, which was to expire on 21.09.2000.

Satoshi pursued this theory and found over the years several errors or possible approaches for attacks. Also his knowledge did not help him, because the Internet was simply too slow to effectively establish a numbering system using this method.

For him came a decisive technological advance with the invention of Napster. Shawn and John Fanning, as well as Sean Parker brought the logical breakthrough that they brought out in 1999 with the implementation almost out of nowhere to the public of the music exchange platform ‚Napster‘. A network, that allows files to be sent directly to another user, with a system that simulates an Internet connection on the Internet. This so-called tunnel is not visible from the outside, and therefore the files could not be intercepted beforehand.

Satoshi came into contact. He was glowing with happiness. His dreams seemed to become reality. At the time, no one was thinking that the network could not prevent swapping files from A to B. But without a directory, in a central location, computers were blind to each other. In

2001 the server with the directory was switched off. Users could no longer locate pieces of music.

Satoshi dismissed the plans from the three founders to send over money-worth files over this network, because it was too easy to turn it off. He also did not like the structure of the data transfer because large files took much longer to transfer and he feared that the system might completely collapse if people start money transfer operations, even if the problem with the server directory could be resolved.

In 2002, the Bit Torrent network appeared which operated similar to Napster, however operated with several servers (Tracker), which independently built their own distribution databases and thus would had no effect in switching off a single tracker. These servers were used so much that the music and film industry had to back down. In addition, this network was used by large companies, because it allowed large amounts of data to be transferred in smaller amounts, thereby making the network considerably faster.

Satoshi took a liking to the idea and worked feverishly on an algorithm that was able to transport files and store them on trackers. With a group of others who were initiated in the procedure, the breakthrough came in 2005, which finally made the basis of his invention possible. A secure decentralised system.

Since the version 4.2.0, which was released in November 2005, supports the reference client, which is the access software for the Bit Torrent network, the tracker less operation, which relies on the Kademlia algorithm. The tracker can be decentralised, as in the Kademlia network, as a distributed hash table from the clients be stored and managed by themselves.

Modern Bit Torrent clients do not need to rely on trackers and work remotely („tracker less"). However, they still use different protocols so that communication between different DHT-based clients is not always possible.

The circle closes

Satoshi sensed that he was not far away from his idea of a safe and secure money transfer. What bothered him was the fact that you could track files in the Bit Torrent network with special software and finding out the IP of the sender. Therefore, by law, the distribution of films and music that are protected by copyright, books etc. have been criminalized. Several agreements were concluded and the person distributing the file should be held liable under the ‚polluter pays' principle. Many were then floo- ded with warnings and claims for damages. That escala- ted so far that law firms developed a business model and put all users under general suspicion. The warnings and following fines led to a lucrative business, because many did not resist and above all the innocent ones simply paid.

The courts eventually stopped this, but that could not be the purpose of a free world. No, he Satoshi, had to develop the existing system. The basics were there, the Internet was fast enough, but now the user was facing a VPN, that was too cumbersome. After all, access to digital money should be as easy as possible and above all free.

He was not seen in the following weeks. He moved away and locked himself away from the outside world. He was programming. He fiddled and calculated and considered how to use the decentralized system with a protocol for everyone. He built more and more computers in the basement. Ultimately, the transmission worked with its own algorithm, but the need for safety left something to be desired.

In an article, he learned that crypto-encryption had reached new dimensions:

According to the way computers work, modern cryptographic methods no longer work with whole letters, but with the individual Bits from the data. This significantly increased the number of possible transformations and also allowed the processing of data that didn't represent a text.

That was the solution, an infinitely scalable crypto-key that can encode to the extent that the human locks himself out.

In the following nights, he modified his algorithm, and after several hours, weeks, months of testing, he had managed to encrypt the file's transmission path outwardly being secure. Not even nine years after its development, it could be hacked. It was a milestone he had found.

But it that was not enough for him, he wanted a different transmission system. Although shredding files brought speed, there were risks inherent in distributing them, individual parts could easily be faked or spied upon.

The solution was to re-encrypt individual blocks separately in the transport path. These containers should then be checked for authenticity by all connected computers. But how?

64

Satoshi is not only a spirit of his time, but was always ahead of others in his way of thinking and has always been a loner. However even the last lone wolf will eventually need something from others. Communication. Through interaction in conversation people are given the key to promoting one's creativity and abstract thinking.

Everybody comes to the point where he wonders if what he is doing is actually correct and plausible in his interpretation. That is, sooner or later we will be forced to look at ourselves reflecting in others. Some say, create a resonance. If esotericism were a single book, then one could summarize the whole thing in one word as RESONANCE.

So we get in contact with other people and present them our way of looking at things. Then we get an answer. Everything in us now begins to form new ways of thinking, be it to explain in more detail to the other person, what you mean yourself (in the year 2017 it looked like this, that you create a one-sided resonance, by imposing your opinion compulsively until it produces a resonance in the opposite side and he agrees after feeling sick and recognizes the one-sided solution as the only truth).

Satoshi had reflected and decided to present his white paper to a few guys. This is not a new form of a kitchen roll and not particularly a white paper, nor does it have anything to do with printer paper.

A white paper represents the essentials of what you have created and is there to help others using and customising your creation for their own needs. Any Lego manual is actually a white paper, as it's just one way to use it, but you can build Lego completely free, something that has nothing to do with the illustration. Nevertheless, the essential of building with the Lego blocks is, being put together with its nubs. The essentials are therefore not changeable.

The perfect system

Safety down to the last details Proof of Work

Satoshi's algorithm, which he then completely provided with a `proof of work procedure`, (oh man, these technical terms that infuriate everyone, you want to understand it, but you just don't get it!) is the Lego piece.

The advancement of technology is thus to create a new construction from the existing Lego pieces, which were originally assembled incorrectly.

So you cannot change the algorithm (the Lego piece symbolically), but rearrange everything or add additions. In computer language this is called OPEN SOURCE.

That's what Satoshi wanted to achieve. The crypto-key cannot change the way a predefined Lego piece looks, but different applications of the algorithm are possible.

Therefore something has to function, it is not so easy to put Lego pieces in the computer even if people have already used the CD drive as a plate salami and coffee cup holder and grandpa is using the iPad as a base for mincing his meat.

Each miner has his own mempool where his own transactions from his wallet will be placed in. All transactions will be copied to each mempool of each miner. So they are working on the same mempool content.

A miner starts to fill this block with a maximum size of

1MB (4200 transactions) from the mempool. Today with the new technology called Segwit transactions in blocks could be compromised and one block can store up between 8400 and 12600 transactions (with so called native SegWit adresses).

Finish filling the blocks the miners send the blocks to the "Proof of work process"

Now the Nodes start to check the blocks for accuracy and if the transactions inside the block fits to the hashcode number of the blocks etc. For this process they create a nonce. The nodes use minimal energy and this energy measure from all 51% of the nodes checking the blocks will be used on the follow up block they create. So the nonce from block 2 will be transformed by a formula into 0s and to the next created block. For example, nonce from checking block 3 will be sent to a specific formula and the result of 0s will be inserted on the hashcode of block 4 and so on.

Every block which is created has his nonce in form of 0's in his hash from the former process.

Once the nodes ended checking with 51% of their power the blocks they return to the miners which created them.

The whole process stops now and the miner start guessing the nonce means they are looking for the number that was sent to the formula to create 0's on their hashcode.

This is the most use of power resources. Because finding a number of million possibilities means the computer produces a lot of energy by guessing. But remind each miner has produced a block. At this moment more than 1 Million miner start guessing the nonce. They are on a run.

The moment one miner found this nonce and it fits into the formula, also the output is equal with the numbers of added 0's to the hashcode of the block, the protocol stops the hunt for the nonce.

The miner who "won" the race will be rewarded with 12.5 BTC (from 2020 on 6.25 BTC be halved each four years) and gets all the transactions fees made in the network during this time as reward for his work.

Now the whole procedure starts from the beginning. Miners starts to fill their own blocks with transactions again.

The whole process from the block creation, checking by nodes, creating a nonce, and hunting the nonce depends on a timeline of 10 minutes.

If computer gets more Hashpower and they will finish under ten minutes the process the protocol makes the nonce from the nodes more difficult by adding more 0's. As a result the hashcode gets more extra 0s and the miner needs more time during the race for bitcoins finding the nonce.

If computer create more Hashpower and they will finish the process in less than ten minutes, the protocol sets the nonce at a more difficult level by adding more 0's. As a result, the hashcode gets more extra 0s and the miners need more time during the race, finding the nonce.

If the miners need more time than ten minutes finding a

block the protocol sets the nonce to an easier level which means there are less 0's added to the hashcode.

That's what we call the Difficulty of the bitcoin network.

Each 2010 founded blocks (which means 14 days) the protocol checks the approximately time the Proof of Work process needs and will change the difficulty.

The more people mine bitcoin, the higher the difficulty will be to give all miners the ability to find a block. Because there is a limited number of BitCoins the more people join mining the more mining results must be divided. In sum they start to buy more and more computers for mining to catch more bitcoins. A never-ending race.

Small terminology:

Normal	In the Blockchain language
Bank	Miner
Post	Node
Bank with post	Fullnode
Nonce	Energy value
Hashpower	Number of guessing attempts that a computer can make in a second
Block Rewards	The number of BitCoins a MINER receives when he validates his block first
MemPool	All open transactions

The vision

Thoughts

Whenever I close my eyes, I see it in front of me. A virus has infected my thoughts and I like it. If that's a kind of disease, I do not want to get well. Many people cannot imagine what a protocol, an algorithm and a concept like this can do, because they are simply facing with a new world.

However, I travel through this world in which yesterday is eternally present and cannot be distorted, even the to-morrow. Our past, the here and now and our future are inextricably intertwined and we create a system that makes our actions with money anonymous and transparent.

The development of humanity has demanded a lot from us and every generation had its own little revolution due to technical advancement.

The question "why?" is a double-edged sword. On the one hand, it is able to destroy people who are unable to extricate themselves from the limitations of thought and passion in our world. This can have different reasons, the loss of a partner, death in the family, a traumatic accident, etc. The emotional cruelty and the question "why?" are diverse. Human life can perish. People are dying of drugs and alcohol. The question "why?" is God's punishment in a believing world.

On the other hand, this question and the eternal conti-nuity of humanity are the engine and the power to create something super-human. "Why?" is the question driving us. We want to know how something works and why it works. The trigger for the researcher's drive is the search for an answer, the answer to the question "why is it that way and not otherwise?"

The discovery of electricity and the invention of the combustion engine are undoubtedly a further development of human intelligence and the question "why?" We are looking for something new and for improvement and we will only succeed if we question things.

It happens when we interact with people and that's what ultimately connects us. We connect with people every day. Often we connect with the same people, but also with other people. Life in itself stands in the focus of connection, because the answer to the question of the why is found in most cases not by itself. But it is the result of a thought process that has grown in our subconscious and now arrives to the surface. We cannot stop thoughts. Once an idea is implanted from our own reflections or through what others have experienced, said or showed us, then the seed is laid.

Thoughts that develop into something great always start small. But you cannot get away from it anymore. They are there and they want to grow. So we have to reflect more and more, get new impressions and seek the conversation with others. The thirst for knowledge of our minds is insatiable driven by the fact that, every new insight, also raises a new "why?"

Satoshi Nakamoto did not give up his quest for perfection in the matter. Certainly, we can and must now make adjustments and improvements from his heritage in order to constantly adapt it to the ever-faster-moving world, but the seed lives on and sprouts.

Many have tried to grow this seed in a different environment, but with little success. Certain plants need certain environments.

BitCoin Blockchain technology needs freedom and peace, because the roots from the seeds embrace our planet. This gift is the ultimate answer to the question "why?"

In a constantly evolving creative process, the question "why?" was transformed into a third force: the question "why not?"

Humanity is always looking for secureness and safety. After all, we are a group of herd animals. Each herd needs a leader, who ultimately controls the rest through life. The herd leader sets the direction. There are many debates about this and of course many counter-voices, ultimately there will always be "the one" who sets the direction.

The problem is, you do not know what price he wants from the herd for doing this job. This can be very pleasant in a humanistic, democratically orientated system. There is usually a standstill and that gives us a reassuring feeling.

It can also be a dictatorship. Fidel Castro is still revered as a folk hero especially after his death, despite all the disadvantages and the associated suffering of the population.

And that's what man does. He says to himself, "why not?"

And seeks justification for it. The "why not?" is the answer to the question of why there are so many cultural differences, why there is, in principle, a vast difference in the views of the Western world and the Eastern world. Why shouldn't it be like that?

We now know that these cultural differences give rise to other thoughts that have often led us to inventions, because they encounter a definitive norm with an abstract approach.

And an abstract technology is the BitCoin Blockchain. We also call it disruptive.

If something new does not replace old views gradually, but radically, irrevocably and suddenly. A lightning strike can be very productive resulting in Luther who came up with his 95 theses. On the other hand, there have been dead players found on football fields.

So we live in a chain linking of circumstances.

Let's say there are only 3 people in the world. Then life becomes quite predictable. The habits of each individual are straightforward. After a period of observation, we begin to know each other, how we react to certain situations, which emotions drive and entice us, and we develop trust, because we understand each other.

If we follow that example and we can live together in peace for several years and everyone has found their task and position in the group, it becomes normality. The way we live and the environment in which we move limit everything we develop now.

One day we see unusual activities in the clearing and when we look to the right, we see two new people. Assuming that we are the only three people in the world, our mind is now being disrupted.

Such serious changes in the current situation cause mistrust and distrust. There are talks. One will say, "Well, let's go to them...", the second will say, "Let them come to us" and the third one will say: "What do they want here, we can do without them!"

Ultimately, it will end up meeting the "newcomers". Fear accompanies us. We deal with the situation distantly. Ideally, we find that the other group is just as unsure.

That leads to a further development. Each unknown group may have had very different experiences. We exchange information through communication. New views are thrown into the room because the two groups may have handled one and the same situation completely differently.

Ideas emerge and possibilities arise from these ideas. If the previous abilities were extended only to a certain circle, the increase, the exchange of opinions with new elements, results in a wealth of possibilities.

All of us are ultimately belonging to a chain and all seven billion people in the world are linked together. Every decision in the past has a point of origin. Whether we are at war or not, whether we are hungry or not, whether we have refugees or not. Each event follows a previous event. A trigger.

If a president gets up on the wrong foot and says to himself: "Today is a good day to erase North Korea", then it will have consequences for the whole world, for every single human being, because they have become part of the world politics.

We're not thinking about accidents today until we've become innocent victims or turned into perpetrators because we overestimated each other. So the circumstances are not only linked to victims and perpetrators, but also to their family and friends. Every event resonates. By serious disasters, people begin to try to prevent negative vibrations. There will be new laws made and so on.

In our example, with 5 people, very clear and understandable, but not with a mass of people who want to regulate themselves. And that's what makes our world sick.

The mass is divided into different cultures and countries, so that groups can be "handled". This inevitably leads to injustice, because what a country sees as good and bad does not coincide with the rest of the masses.

But we are actually like the blocks on the Blockchain. We are different, but we know about the others. We notice if something goes wrong. We see the injustices, and the ‚proof of work' is ultimately our feelings.

It does not matter which country we are in. No matter what skin colour people have or what views they represent. Everyone is ultimately an animal belonging to the human species. This means, in the radical consequence, that we all define ourselves through our feelings.

A hungry lion is defined by a primal instinct; he must eat, to survive. So to get his food his own life becomes secondary in dangerous situations.

The human being knows these feelings in the same way and will eventually eat snails, grasshoppers and ants. If he is a little tougher, also slaughter animals and barbecue them on the open fire.

The most civilized citizen will become a wild beast in extreme circumstances, since our natural instinct is to secure and defend our survival.

Ultimately we are what we think.

According to nature we know that every new life is linked to the old, and from here new life arises. Our world is the perceived reality of the mass and we often feel alienated.

So if the algorithm of the BitCoin Blockchain were feeling emotions, it would feel "alienated" by the protocol.

Our medical advances have come a long way for those people who have access to it. Especially, for the rulers of a herd. Because even if the herd suffers, she will do the best possible to keep her ruler alive and healthy.

This is based on the fear of self-responsibility, which is dedicated to the question "why?" in the negative. "Why did our leader die? How shall we continue?"

Taking responsibility is therefore genetic and evolutionary and only reserved for a few. This is explained by observing the animal world. An anthill with 200,000 ants is completely organized from the first to the last ant. If our postal service and logistics functioned that way today, there would be no lost letters, no lost luggage on a flight.

So we also try to implement ideas from the animal world for our own needs. This shows us that we are in a constant flow with nature and ourselves. One cannot exist without the other. Unfortunately we destroy nature, which we depend on.

Children are the worst. When growing up, we try things out like jumping on a snail; we torture ants with magnifying glasses roasting them alive. We crush beetles and suck up spiders and house dust mites.

So we deliberately intervene in the cycle of life and forget that the animal called "human species" is also destroying his own existence. Every day we try to destroy the green lungs of the earth. And there she is again, the painful question of "Why?"

It's the greed for money. We cannot eat money, but we can define ourselves with it. Definition means being envious or patronising. To begrudge someone success or to envy him is, of course, the highest form of recognition. Every believer then would have to be jealous of his creator. Everybody should think for themselves, if there is something like that or not. For many people, an idea that changes everything is a divine inspiration, to me; it is just the quintessence out of trial and error.

Mahatma Gandhi was not a divine creation, but the natural result of consequence and counteraction. You can mistreat people, but at some point, this will end. The mind is always stronger than the flesh, they say so nicely. It is the will and the vision that make us great.

Visions are not an engine, visions are, almighty. A vision feeds on the positive success and response in a very short time. A vision does not come from experience, but is the lightning strike that hits you when you least expect it.

Satoshi Nakamoto had a vision. He put his vision into action. If money is the evil of the world, then I'll make the money a little better. I'll make sure the money does not get any more expensive. In a system where money is subject to natural growth, everyone can participate.

From Satoshi Nakamoto's vision I developed my vision. And as I experience it, it is like a large-scale fire, which causes upheavals.

From the legacy of Nakamoto we have received a weapon that enforces justice and equality. Transparency and effi-
i
ciency at the same time. Man can use this weapon against poverty. 1.5 billion people are, so to speak, "unbanked". They are the collateral damage from our affluent society, which, however, no longer takes care of them. Human greed destroys many, many lives every day.

Going back to nature: animals hunt sensibly and ecological. Everything that comes and goes was a harmonious cycle of food and needs. Man has broken and destroyed this cycle.

The only natural enemy that man still has is himself. In five minutes I can disassemble myself or destroy someone else. People who have nothing kill for money. Those who have nothing to lose can only win. Every day thousands of people experience this. War is the normal everyday life for many people. Children shoot with guns killing others. In moderate countries, the kids play war on the computer.

It is the primal instinct we have. We are predators, but we have civilised ourselves. There are two types of human beings: ones who give and others that take.

I can say thank you to nature, for my life and my food, or I can see it as a product of excess and throw it away. I am not really happy with that. Throwing away leftovers when eating, everybody has experiences this.

Interestingly, Nakamoto's legacy is a freely available. Everyone can use it. There are no rules, you cannot turn it off or delete it. The BitCoin and the Blockchain will out-live everything, because it is the eternity, the present and the past in one entity.

If somebody has physically created the Holy Trinity, then it was Satoshi.

And that is what bothers everyone. Governments and their finances systems. Power is always a concentration of faith and money. Where faith has no money, it can spread, but it will not reach the mass. Where money is without faith, there are no values.

The Rothschilds realised that. We have created a system that dictates trust. By regulation! In many countries currency exchange is not possible or only in limited quantities.

If the value of money is too high for many leaders, there could be a shift of power in the people's favour, which could through sovereignty override the existing system.

To avoid this, values are artificially regulated. Central increases of currencies by purchase or central depreciation by flooding the market with new money.

The principle, *I give you a loan and you pay it back to me in instalments* makes it easy to afford something, but becomes outdated, for example I buy an iPhone 7 today and a month later the iPhone 8 surprisingly comes on the market, an individual will find a way to get the iPhone 8. In most cases, the owner has to sell his iPhone 7 below value and add the difference in price on the purchase of the iPhone 8. This will be refinanced.

The debts have thus increased significantly. Since our own devices have an automatic expiration date, we are forced to buy new ones. The new washing machine, the new car, the new bike, replacing the broken TV and without a mobile phone you would be living cut off from the rest of the world.

Debts are financed by debt and a cycle of dependency is created. The debtor is committed to a minimum repayment in order to serve the consumption cycle.

Satoshi has now found a way in which debts do not arise, or rather, are not provided. Credit accounts. With BitCoins, the owner regains control over his money and can use his money worldwide without any restrictions. No one can block his accounts and nobody can take his money. Even not a judge's order. Because nobody knows that someone owns BitCoins.

The privacy of the individual must be protected and treated with respect. Once you've gone through the security checks in Atlanta, you definitely have no free life left. From now on, the NSA can trace you around the world.

To get a connecting flight, you have to plan 2 hours time for a flight from Costa Rica. At first you are going through some simpler controls and instructions, then you become a victim of Borderland Security.

For Europeans with ESTA it is really hell. Before you even come to America, you have to fill out a $ 14 online form. The checking of this form takes 3 days, you then get a number, with this number you have to check online if it has been approved. You do not get an email.

Then you have to fill in a declaration during the flight to America and sign that you do not bring anything illegal and answer several questions. Among other things, the address where you come from and where you want to go. You already did that when checking in at the airport. Double check is better, in the meantime you could have bought something in the plane, which does not belong in America.

At the airport itself then one goes with his electronic pass to a machine. Reinstate the passport there. Confirm the scan, and then scan all the fingers of the left hand, then the right one. Then a picture is taken.

And now it gets really insane. You go into a queue to get to the pass control 10 meters away. The officer is either moody or nice. So show your passport. Leave fingerprints of both hands on his device and because it's so much fun; take another picture.... You could have gotten a beard unexpectedly from waiting so long, that covers the whole face or form women it could happen that her make-up slips and the person behind it looks different,... By the way, at the machine you get a photo, which one also shows the inspector here. Then it goes to full check - shoes off, unpack laptop, empty pockets and trough the body scanner, if necessary, a drug test is taken with stripes on the clothes. Then you go through the next control and leave the photo from the machine here.

We are only talking about changing to another plane within the same airport.

Counter-terrorism is nice when terror starts within the rules.

I think whoever went through that will understand why Satoshi Nakamoto dreamed of a borderless world.

Anyway the years 2016 and 2017 are sacrificed to the control mania and the free world has to hurry to get all the assets in BitCoins.

Even if you can only convert a certain amount monthly. Along with the time something will be gathered. Or you can buy your BitCoins on the platform localbit-coins.com or bitsquare.com.

Yes, there is still a free world, which is implemented by the supporters of decentralization on high-tech level. In 2017, there will even be a system on the market that makes it impossible to track information, as this information is exchanged with any number of people.

If you are in Europe, can you say ad hoc which country is pictured on the back of your 1 Euro coin? Certainly not and otherwise you should think about whether everything is still all right. So ultimately you are only thinking about the value, being 1 Euro.

It's the same with BitCoins. These have a kind of serial number because of the crypto key. If the serial numbers are mixed up, then only recipients and senders can know from the entry in the cashbook what has happened. The already sent BitCoin no longer corresponds to the serial number that has arrived at the recipient.

A follow-up with the so-called perfected tumbler procedure is impossible. Another possibility, with the somewhat unusual name Mimblewimble (the French-speaking Lord Voldemort sends greetings) compresses several BitCoins and separates them randomly at the end to recipient addresses. This guarantees complete invisibility.

Satoshi Nakamoto must have guessed that he had to keep his program open to developers, so-called Open Source Software. Apart from that he was very far-sighted. It is impossible to hack the BitCoin network.

This is just as sure as you, after being at the airport in Atlanta, certainly not being a free man anymore.

Smart Contracts

The world is becoming fairer.

Our world was built according to certain conditions. And where better to observe this than in an Excel spreadsheet. Many people have worked with Excel before. Here we can create tables and calculate in the table. For example, we can write invoices, build a database from which Excel can extract the information it needs. You can enter 21 as an article number and Excel automatically enters the position and the price, calculating the total price and the VAT.

All this is entered with the commands: if, then, and, or and some more.

Our whole life evolves from such terms.

Laws, our communication and our actions are ultimately shaped by action and reaction.

Satoshi knew that smart contracts existed back in the 1990s. He already implemented the function to set up these Smart Contracts in the main program. But took them out again, because he thought, you could possibly infiltrate a virus into the BitCoin network.

In addition, the company bithalo.org developed applications for the Smart Contracts in the BitCoin Blockchain and it is now possible to generate decentralized marketplaces, job boards and decentralized emails. A program like a building kit. The nice thing is, none of these applications can be turned off.

That's because the BitCoin is ultimately just a file, just like a Smart Contract. The Proof Of Work is the same, and now the exchange is documented by a token. A token is a file that contains information. For example, about certain properties. Tokens can also act as digital stocks if they are holding the stock information.

So one can then exchange BitCoins for tokens, and in the public cashbook thus generating the Smart Contract.

With Smart Contracts, it is now possible to turn off any intermediary agency, the central bank, the notary for certain tasks, the lawyer for certain things, the middleman, etc.

From it a DAO can be derived. This is not some secret code, nor is it a Chinese or Japanese proverb tattooed on parts of a body (I have never seen a Chinese or a Japanese tattooing the words 'I love you' on his back, in our language or any other quotes).

DAO stands for Decentralized Anonymous Organisation - De-central Anonymous Organisation.

This type of project can take over various tasks, such as collecting and managing money. You can create projects that are then processed fully automatically. Collect donations, implement contracts and execute, for example. There are people who believe that they can more or less replace governments and put their trust in the mathematics and logic of the machine to make decisions with no falsification.

Let's take the example of a car. With a Smart Contract and a decentralized Blockchain, as well as the BitCoin as a means of payment, I can build a driverless taxi from Google car, which responds to a call and the language issuing its commands.

If anyone came up with the idea to join them, just call the taxi and it will calculate the best route and then drive there.

Should the service reminder come on to refill oil or simply refuel, the taxi will drive to the filling station or service workshop independently and will pay for itself with Bit-Coins.

If you build up a fleet of such taxis now, then you have a taxi company as a DAO, which operates completely, without human intervention, and gets on with its business.

Humanity is about to restart, but only if the normal person takes on this technique. It is important to understand the difference between distributed Blockchain networks and central systems.

BitCoin vs. Government vs. FinTec

The race against digital enslavement.

It's late on my flight from Costa Rica home to Germany, where my current, permanent residence is. I have taken with me many new impressions from conversations and encounters. Time here reflects on the events, and considering all the talking that has emerged, new connections that have been made, I think rightly that there is hope. Hope for a life in a better world.

People are beginning to understand that they must escape a system of systematic surveillance and financial extortion. Also, many are beginning to realise that you cannot get rich overnight, but all the more so that the counter value of traditional money is dwindling. To offset this, England has actually taken the path of „Brexit" and has broken away from the European Union.

Everywhere there are efforts to escape the old monetary system. The BitCoin breaks down capital limits and changes our society more than we can imagine.

But governments and banks are not sleeping and they are now, after a deep sleep, trying to catch up, which turns out to be a grave of millions.

Questions and Answers

Can a government and the financial community stop BitCoin?

The answer is no (you were not expecting anything else were you? But the question "why?" nibbles at you now). The BitCoin network consists of 1.6 million computers at the time of writing this book. They're not in one place, not as if you drop a bomb and then it's all over.

We have a mix of big mining farms. Here companies have started to build up a lot of mining computers. The processing power of these computers are brought together enabling computers to do much more guesswork for hashing rewards trough mining.

As a result, China now has 70 percent of all mining farms and most of the 12.5 BTC blocks a day go there. Outside of China, there are also mining farms that are very lucrative, e.g. in Iceland. Computer freaks operate the remaining computers, so-called solo miners who just want to participate and support the network.

The mining farms account for about 1 million of the computers and the 'other' 600,000 computers. These are somewhere in the basement, in the attic, in the garage or anywhere else, by someone like us. It could be your neighbour. Or it could be you yourself. Simply download the program from the Internet and get started.

The government would have to turn off all computers. One working computer is enough to restore the whole system. So you see, the governments of this world have no possibility to end it.

There have been attempts to ban this in China, Russia, Venezuela, Argentina and also in Germany, and people have been imprisoned who have been mining, and China stating the death penalty for those involved.

What happens then? Absolutely nothing, people just carry on. The need for people to act rather than think, when their own money becomes less and less valuable, living costs rise, quality of life is reduced to a minimum.

What if governments shut down the exchanges?
First, the price would shoot up. Demand for the existing access is then huge.

You can use BitCoins like Fiat money. You create a wallet with a sample amount of $ 100. Then print the related private key (pin / tan) on a piece of paper. Now give this 36-digit number to someone else. He goes into his wallet and imports the number by typing it there. Now he has the $ 100 in BitCoins, and he gives you the amount in cash.

The localbitcoins.com page is a directory of people who trade BitCoins for cash. In countries where the regulati-ons of exchanges etc, increase, the use of local BitCoins increases at the same proportion. The advantage is that you remain anonymous.

In Germany, local BitCoins is only accessible via VPN. Bit-Coin-Treff.de fulfils the same goal.

Before you lie dead in corner here is a practical tip:

Meet at public places, i.e. cafés, restaurants, market-places, etc. Do not take money or BitCoins with you at the first meeting. Do not mention it. If you have a bad guy sitting opposite to you, you can check him out without anything-negative happening.

So we've learned one thing, that turning off the exchanges does not work.

Preventing BitCoins and their use is no longer possible because the whole thing has simply become too big.

The pure demand and global trading with BitCoins cannot be stopped, not now, nor in the future.

Technology and speed. Is it not too slow when millions use the network?

The BitCoin Blockchain has been designed from the outset that it can be made faster. Satoshi Nakamoto was aware that to maintain the system the computers could not withstand the rapid increase in users. In fact, we have a lot more users today for the technology than computers can process. In comparison:

Visa can process 1,680 transactions per second

Master/Visa can process up to 300,000 transactions per second

BitCoin Blockchain can currently process 7 transactions per second

What effects does this have?
Currently, sending BitCoins to the receiver takes up to 3 hours. That's not much, considering that one waits in conventional banks 1 - 3 days. And investors who natur-

ally want to advance the technology so that the BitCoin value rises also support BitCoins.
BitCoin users are rapidly increasing worldwide, so it's natural that something should happen.

As a result, more and more people are paying higher fees for a preferred transfer. In practice, you will then be asked in your wallet when completing the transaction, how much in fees you want to pay. These are usually already stated. The Blockchain is therefore in its speed a lucrative business model for the miners.

What options are there for making the Blockchain faster, and is there already a decision as to which system will be implemented?

There were originally only two options:

Seggregated Wittness (SEGWIT for short)

Adjusts the size of the blocks (boxes of transactions)

In the past, a huge dispute broke out in the BitCoin community. Ostensibly it looked like everyone had a different view on which system would be the safest. However, it quickly became apparent that the defenders from the each side were only concerned about the loss of fees.

Just quickly to explain that SegWit is able to transfer transactions to another blockchain connected to the BitCoin Blockchain. That's what you call a sidechain. However, the company SegWit assumes that 95 percent of all computers can activate the program.

Of course, the inventors of SideChain and SegWit also want to earn on the transactions.

On the other hand, miners on the network earn less when transactions are run through SegWit.

In the weeks that followed, we saw a fight of vanities with prominent representatives of the BitCoin scene, who were actually arguing about fee distribution.

The arguments for and against a solution became more and more crazy. The debate has a drawback for that reason alone: the solution of enlarging the blocks requires creating a new operating system. This is called a hard fork. This is similar to the fact that Windows 8 eventually became Windows 10. In our case you would then have two blockchains with the BitCoin.

Now users can decide whether to use the old software or the new one. There are still users of Windows 7 and Windows 98 today.

If the case of a hard-fork occurring, the price for a BitCoin would have been cut in half. A lot of people who work with BitCoin would lose a lot of money every day.

The two sides are well aware of the situation. Their advocates are more interested in their own profiling in the discussion, instead of quick solutions.

Which solution has been agreed on?
The debate ultimately resulted in several development teams working on different solutions and finding a consensus on SegWit and the possibility of sidechains.

The following alternative solutions are available and will be activated during the year:
'Tumbler'

This project is intended to make the transactions more anonymous than they already are, and it works very well. As a spin off, Tumbler also uses a SideChain and thus the BitCoin transactions are much faster anyway.

Extension Blocks - SegWit 2MB

The company purse.io has found a way to create extension blocks. These blocks manage to double the number of transactions in a block through a special compression method.

Bcoin
The mining company BTC.Com mined the first so-called BCoin. This is a block that was not created with the original software by Satoshi Nakamoto, but with a reprogramming of the core program.

The computers with the old software inevitably have to check the newly created blocks. However, a computer with this new program does not need to check the block of an old computer. The new software is also able to activate SegWit and sidechains.

What would simply happen is a so-called USER ACTIVATED SOFT FORK.

This means that users will automatically start the new program and reboot their computer.

The old programs have to have their blocks (boxes with transactions) tested by at least 51 percent of all computers connected to the network for correctness.

If 51 percent of the computers were now converted to the new software by User Soft Fork (which is as if you have Office installed and now comes the message that you have to restart your PC), then the blocks from the other computers are no longer being checked because the new software simply invalidates these blocks.

This indirect blackmail and the indication that the company that wrote this software wants to return to low transaction costs (mining fees) and end the dispute in favour of the users of BitCoins silenced the debate in April 2017.

Grinding their teeth, everyone has now agreed to activate SegWit and not give a hard fork a chance.

The benefits of SegWit, such as connecting SideChains or creating extra blocks are just too big and you can now increase the frame size of a block without a hard fork.

The agreement provides that the implementation must have taken place by October 2017 at the latest.

Who decides what to do in the BitCoin Blockchain world? The magic word is called BLOCKCRAZY

Everyone can load the program for the BitCoin Blockchain, the Core, simply on his or her computer, and you're ready to vote. If you want to save on the high electricity costs for mining, just put a tick in the program on NODE.

In this mode you will not find any BitCoins and no building of any blocks. The NODES serve, as described, only the logistics in the network, so they are what's called the streets and traffic lights of the data communication.

The protocol has specified that the nodes are eligible to vote.

So that means anyone who runs a miner with a node (full-node) or just a node.

But there are also miners who only pack boxes, etc., but are not configured as nodes, to reduce traffic and thus save costs. These are not entitled to vote. Not even Cloudminer, which are people who do not have their own computers, but have leased the service and thus participate in the profits of those who hold the miner.

You get asked a question in your core and you answer yes or no. This yes or no is information that is attached to the hash code of the next generated block. A statistic program now reads this information and then says, for example, block number 230,000 had an addition that is correct for SegWit (yes) or is against it (no).

It is therefore possible to build through this voting system:

*A decentralized anonymous organizations (DAO)_*

Therefore, the Node owner votes on a certain date, when the decision must be YES or NO to reach a consensus.

Here and now

Will the future be as hoped?

It is 12:30 o'clock the alarm rings without mercy and the last night flows into the noon of the next day. Wake up! Terrible thought. What in the world have I done wrong to get up in such a world every day?

Katrin is 45 years old and works as a cleaner. After the divorce and with the "legacies", as they say, with children aged 15 and 16, she is forced to make a living in a reality of daily work, in a job with a lot of overtime and little pay-ment. She needs 45 minutes to get through busy traffic in the morning and on the way back as well. Even at week-ends, only having the Sunday to relax and sometimes not even that, Sunday shopping is also on the agenda.

Some refer to this as a hamster wheel and euphemistic people regard this from the hamster's point of view as a career ladder. For Katrin it is a nightmare par excellence. On the one hand, she is grateful for the work, because in her region jobs are not easy to get, on the other hand, there is the desire for freedom and self-determination. Saturday night, like yesterday, she is off and has a hell of a party. This can lead to waking up somewhere else at noon. There are plenty of excuses and having children is a good way to fend off the Casanovas because they are not the best choice to bring up kids, and for them saying 'goodbye' politely is the best they can do. Her thoughts, however, revolved around another conversation. One of her "best" friends wanted to take her out to a talk about

97

"BitCoins". She had heard about the Satoshi School and it was supposed to be the only school in the world to really honestly explain about crypto currencies. (was not Crypton the stuff that makes Superman suffer unwillingly?)

Real enthusiasm looks different; this 'best friend' got her involved months ago in a so-called pyramid scheme (also called Ponzi or Multi level marketing). At that time she found the saying "...we do our job in summer..." from her friend still funny. Today, and 5,000 Euros less, it is a cynical joke, if you are looking in the holiday industries winter catalogue.

She had put all her savings in the promises of a new coin, a new digital currency that promised to overshadow BitCoin, which is too slow and outdated.

Today, Katrin feels outdated herself. And now this. The invitation came by phone and her friend sounded very factual, not the enthusiasm she had had before. Rachel had lost nearly $ 100,000. Time to have a closer look, after her previous disaster she did not want to make mistakes again. Katrin agreed and that changed her life.

In a room somewhere in Frankfurt, a group of people were meeting and wanting nothing more than to save the world. Their leader, a longhaired bomb plotter, mother-in-law's nightmare (life-artists are always a thorn in the eye of society), is giving a talk on BitCoins. His fans are already sitting and hanging on to every word from his tongue. They use the occasion to infuse their ideas. The discussion took place. Projects were talked about, also the future of humanity. If this was not the Satoshi School's Kick Off Meeting, it would be easy to believe that this was some sort of esoteric movement with a banker financing the incense sticks.

Groups of people came together to teach humanity about BitCoin, courses like the one booked by Katrin with her friend Rachel. Training and content were perfected, and after a 2-day seminar Katrin returned home and for the first time in her sad existence, after her husband cheated on her with the neighbour, in their own marriage bed, something like hope came over her... The seminar was marked by a vision. This vision was so straightforward, consistent and so authentic and vividly transmitted by the Satoshi School that Katrin decided to begin a training course to become part of the school and to teach people about BitCoins, showing them how to achieve financial self-determination and freedom. Katrin wants to be part of seeing people regain control of their lives and creating a better world.

The last few years have nearly broken Katrin spiritually in her struggle to survive but many others as well. The numbers of mentally ill people today is higher than the number of traffic victims or traffic accident victims with injuries.

In Germany it is embarrassing to admit that you are going to a psycho doc. The people here are, as far as the subject is concerned, still in the stone age, believing they are not ticking properly or being put in an institution (no doubt some government officials and a few bankers would be better off there, there they cannot harm mankind).

But it is there to support and help to find a remedy, because manpower must be sustained or who is going to pay for everything?

We then elegantly call it burn out syndrome. Woman gone, job gone, seized account, no idea what happens next, knocked out from the system. Burn out and off you go to the psycho doctor. 3 - 6 weeks special leave in a health care institution.

The employer is happy, when you return freshly motivated for a few more years with new drive to endure the madness. Everything will be fine.

The wish to free yourself from this situation lures people alike into more dubious things, such as multilevel marketing. Right now, with everyone interested in BitCoin, swindlers and con men in the digital world have an easy time. Thanks to the discovery of NLP (neuro-linguistic programming also better known as brainwashing), every average intelligent person is now able to get a host of idiots together to believe that they are actually mining crypto currency. Meaning that we have developed a 'proof of' ... procedure and you can already buy "pre distributed" coins etc.

At the moment people are putting a lot of money into this hope and are often unable to convince new people to do the same. So they tell dubious stories and wonder why, after the whole show has collapsed, that they themselves become victims of shit-storms.

It could be so easy. Just buy a few bit coins and don't touch them... The value increases continuously. From $ 450 in March 2016 to $ 1,200 in March 2017.

It is in the nature of things. Unfortunately, like Katrin and her friend, most people have no idea and it does not seem unusual to them if a web site makes promises like "... 7 BitCoins in 2 weeks." Then one checks out a few webinars from some NLP zombies and you have been perfectly conditioned to invest in and gamble on your money.

And then when the phone rings and the sentence comes... "I have to show you something, that is not explainable on the phone" At that point you realise, you have been completely fooled, especially working in a call centre yourself and explaining to others on the telephone.

But how could it be otherwise, instead of thinking for yourself, you can trust your best friend, he has to know it, and if you're unlucky, the money is gone and your best friend is as well. There are enough of those types.

If you go back to the question whether the future will be better: certainly not this way. It would be too easy. Worth mentioning, however, that as a result, many people do already own BitCoins and are therefore quite open to visit a course to find out why it is a currency and how it benefits the world.

We have a long way to go. The FinTec world celebrates itself with new achievements, using more and more money, and then realising that it does not work. Meanwhile, there are growing reports that this new type of technology is unlikely to be suitable for banks, as they cannot meet their needs and with a large number of applications it simply breaks down.

That's no wonder, because at the moment, leading programmers on the BitCoin Blockchain say that only 60 percent of them have been researched. And yes, we are experiencing new wonders from the BitCoin Blockchain world almost every day or did you know that the BitCoin Blockchain can also be established via radio? The core program has a 5 GHz transmission. So called ad-hoc networks. Did you know that a Browser is installed in the core and that you could also create and store Internet pages in the BitCoin network?

This is not an easy task because transactions do not store content, except for a brief use. However, you can create so called tokens (value containers) that receive data and then execute them.

So the world is constantly reinventing itself, and so are the people. The speed of it presented here is not easy for many. Keeping pace in this world of technology is a supreme discipline. The interesting thing about our present time is that we can see a lot of developments being made on the BitCoin Blockchain, which makes it much easier for us to live and work together. Be it the money business or automated processes with smart contracts.

8 years of development now begins to show the performance and the effective added value and benefits.

The future has begun

BitCoins cannot be stopped, and the rapid increase in people who convert their common currencies into BitCoins is growing rapidly. Twice this amount is currently set at 2 years and there are currently around 30 million users worldwide. The economic crises in the world (Brexit, Greece, Argentina, Africa, etc.), the loss of confidence in traditional currencies and the depreciation of currencies due to rising inflation are leading to the revaluation of BitCoin.

From a mathematical point of view, Europe is already broke, before it started, and this is where BitCoin will really do well. Europeans are still doing good, however there are many business leaders who are currently having second thoughts and thinking about alternatives, which leads them somewhere along the line to the BitCoin.

With the founding of Satoshi School, the world's only school for BitCoins with its decentralization and BitCoin Blockchain technology, a new global player has emerged to bring people back into the forefront.

With all the technical discussions, it's easy to forget that the mission is to bring people closer together again. Globalization is meant to add value to people in general, and instead we have crises over crises.

The Satoshi School is working on the implementation of its system and more and more people daily follow the philosophy and conviction that a better world is accomplished through BitCoins and the decentralized BitCoin Blockchain. A good example is Japan, where the BitCoin is slowly replacing the Yuan, which is suffering from depreciation.

There are now 260,000 places in Japan and more than 600,000 worldwide where BitCoin is accepted. The number of dealers that accept bit coins ranges from the airport car park in Denver to electronics retailers.

With BitCoins you can buy anything you need, directly or

through services, from a car to a houseboat - from food to services. Today, we can see donation projects that were previously unthinkable.

People are able to donate a tenth of a penny, since the BitCoin is scalable to the eighth point, this smallest unit is also called Satoshi.

For example, China has lost its monopoly on trading tea to Blockchain after 150 years, as the businesses are now running through Smart Contracts and BitCoins, which means tea can be sold without China acting as a middleman. As a result, we can see a lot of tea coming onto the market at better conditions for everyone involved.

We have begun to value gold and diamonds, which cannot be falsified with a certificate in the Blockchain and to determine their origin and distribution. The BitCoin Blockchain allows the poorest to order from the web shop Amazon, they would not be able to use their money otherwise. And there are still many projects under development or running.

2030 is close at hand; all we have to do is bring the governments and the financial world into the secure decentralized BitCoin Blockchain. This allows citizens for the first time in history to ensure transparency in the elected government.

2030 can come, the future orientate to that. And we, as small house dust mites have then occupied the universe for peace and a better world.

The opponents of the free world

The power of evil.

The circle of men in fine thread took place this time in an unusual place. Far away from the centres of the world, in a small restaurant somewhere in the mountains. Although the sun was shining that day and the blue sky could not have been better, a subdued mood spread. These are the places where you can go to discuss your secrets with a select circle of people. There is no Internet, no mobile telephone network; you are on your own.

The advantage of such places comes from the fact that today no one gets along without Internet or his smart phone for a long time; the idea of missing something is just too evident. This in turn means that you want the outcome to be united as quickly as possible so as not to have to hold a follow-up meeting again, in the same place.

Bernard Trechoít liked the idea of doing one hundred percent business and looking logically at his life so far, how can one doubt it, he has being crowned with success.

His fortune had unbelievably increased in the last 12 months.

New laws and strong demands for renewable energy, crude oil, etc. Due to these crisis points, his constant investment and assurance with his bank in investment models have done well. There is no income return, but final commission. And there is plenty of that.

But he and his bank colleagues face a threat. In his lecture in the morning he brought this fact to the point.

BitCoin is the little man's bazooka. With this new universal means of payment, one of the most important core businesses of a bank will disappear in the future. The private customer business. Of all the models, the bank charges are profitable for the bank.

And behold, out of nowhere a currency was created that is not issued by banks, but by computers. And worst of all, you cannot turn it off or put it under pressure. People use the system. Much worse, it has become a valid currency in many countries. In Japan it has even become the main currency.

Bernard is scared of this. A world he cannot control. Where he cannot turn the adjustment screws, as it was previously possible.

The select circle of honourable gentlemen including Jack of the Banco Nationale, as a lightweight, heads of governments, managers and security service here are representatives of the old world and they have only one goal, how can you stop this madness and make sure the power stays where it should stay, because if you have no power, all the lovely boat cruises of their lives are worthless. The BitCoin founders with their "New World" crap, now though it appears, they also have a considerable sum of money.

Behind closed doors, they will decide in the next few hours to use alternative coins, such as Ethereum and Ripple, and to invest money and put expertise in their development.

106

For Bernard this is a good way to position himself.
After the meeting, he will have gathered together another
100 million dollars to share in the dream of having his
own Blockchain and the innovations of the FinTec industry, and then he will show everyone what he is capable of,
once you let him. Then he'll lock away these longhaired
computer nerds out there and shut down and destroy that
thing called BitCoin.

For centuries, his ancestors and now he himself worked at
these traditional houses and institutions. He and the assembled heads of state from America, Germany, France,
Italy, India, China and Russia will find a way, whatever
the cost to reassert the traditional values. He wouldn't
be responsible for trampling on his legacy and watching
a redistribution of values being carried out by a few crazy
computer freaks.

Michael Stephen and he recently took part on a cruise
with one of the most luxurious ships in the world. The
Coinsbank had sent the invitation, one of the largest exchanges in the crypto currencies.

There was indeed a representative of the BitCoin world.
And he very impressively spoiled their mood. A live hack
of Ethereum was the consequence of the presentation
from the BitCoin people. This resulted in the course of Ethereum and Ripple shooting into the basement for a short
time. Yes, they were all scared, because FinTec is the next
"big thing" for trading and fixed assets, and that's why
you have Ethereum and Ripple, nobody wants BitCoin.

At this meeting they will create regulations, they were

107

sure, to stop the BitCoin. No one can be made a fool of, especially not by such nerds.

Yes, the opponents of BitCoin and the BitCoin Blockchain do not have it easy. The power of evil is in every BitCoin.

They have not realised that they have become the enemy of the people. These people do not fit into the scheme of a new world of decentralization and so they have to give way. Sooner or later.

Those who do not keep up with the time, will disappear with time.

The FinTec industry is devouring more and more money without profit. To date, there has been no significant technical progress in the FinTec projects. They are running on the spot. Many conferences are held, new projects are celebrated, new ICOs are presented and all have one thing in common: the implementation fails due to the non-feasibility and erroneous implementations, so it is an easy thing to hack and destroy these pretty central solutions. What's missing is innovation!

We can see the desperate attempts of the FinTec industry trying to follow the development of the BitCoin Blockchain. Meanwhile, the Blockchain of BitCoin is many times faster and will be even more so. By the end of 2017, it will be up to 100,000 transactions per second.

Everything will stay different. And that's good.

Experiences from everyday life and the Satoshi School

How the world experiences BitCoin.

Let's do a little round trip through the past and see if the BitCoin has achieved anything at all.

As an adventurous person who loves variety and gets bored quickly when routine arises, you, revered (or strayed?) reader, can surely imagine that the subject of BitCoin and the evolution of money is an exciting theme.

Especially since it has its own explosive power. Never before have all areas of life been so thoroughly shaken up by such an innovation. The Internet was only the beginning. It lays in the nature of things to hear from one side about, but it's quite another thing to make a picture for yourself.

When I started the school, I did not know what to expect. I wanted to create a school where true knowledge is taught. The problem I saw was that people were completely misinformed. How could they have known better? In recent years, multilevel marketing (also called Ponzi or pyramid scheme) came quickly on the scene; you can earn a lot of money from people with a lack of knowledge.

For me, it was clear that you have to go where people are open to the topic. It quickly became clear that there was a need in Greece and so the first on-site training started.

Comprehensive matter poses the challenge of choosing

the right content so that people do not fall asleep during the lecture, and that they can present a lively topic. The first course began on Crete, it became clear that I had taken the right path and interest increased so much that more courses followed.

What made Greece so interesting was the fact that the Grexit had taken place and the capital restrictions can be easily and safely avoided with BitCoins.

Of course you cannot easily convert 50,000 Euros into BitCoins in Greece today. Infrastructures have to be created. The advantage in Crete is the fact that Local BitCoins works very well there. This is a meeting place on the Internet, where you can meet with fellow human beings and exchange BitCoins for cash. That makes things easier and safer.

In Greece, about 0.25 percent of residents now use BitCoins and every day the number increases.

The motto is 'to clarify' and it works. The BitCoin world is full of myths and misinformation, so there is a great need for education. In search of a suitable solution we came up with a concept of not having the school in one place but to offer courses that take place at different locations.

If you run the only school that deals with the philosophy behind BitCoin, fundamentally changing the world with Smart Contracts and the benefits of using BitCoins as a world currency, then it expands.

I quickly realized that there are not too many experts who feel like changing the world in a positive way. As
110

a result, I was honoured in 2017 as Trainer Excellence and even listed in the German Dictionary of Speakers. There was no better springboard to publicise BitCoin and its capabilities and bring it to the world. Today I give speeches at major Blockchain conferences, in addition to working as a seminar leader.

One of the most important conferences of the time is the Coinsbank Cruise. A gathering of Blockchain experts from the FinTec world, and when you picture a decentralised world that's not just about greed, you can meet some pretty irritated people here.

Due to my increasing popularity and my contrary opinions, I have now been invited to India and to a further boat cruise between Japan and China.

After being in Haiti, Puerto Rico, Bermuda, and New York, I can draw the following conclusion:

People are open to new things and ready to reach out over their habits.

You can also see the gap between rich and poor. While the poorer people see the BitCoin as a stable asset, which gives by its rise in price even the smallest more prosperity, the wealthy see it as an investment.

Due to the fact that the wealthy buy up BitCoin, you can see a steady increase in price in the exchange Fiat - BitCoin.

Due to the rapid development and worldwide acceptance of BitCoin as a means of payment, we will see it in the next few years replace many currencies. The big ones in the business, like Bill Gates, Richard Branson, etc, all believe this will happen.

Due to more and more technical innovations and the increase of the network speed behind the BitCoin, the Blockchain, new possibilities are opening up.

The BitCoin Blockchain makes the manual administration in many areas superfluous. You could close the field of accountancy and dissolve most administrations. The Smart Contract takes over the role of the clerk, etc., and the BitCoin Blockchain with the payment medium BitCoin does the rest on its own in an absolutely secure environment.

I have experienced a lot on my travels that people want to use this decentralized innovation, but for different reasons.

The spectrum ranges from a distrust in the system, pessimistic views on a guaranteed value and undistorted proof of transactions.

In countries where the normal currency is plagued by hyperinflation, the BitCoin is taken as a substitute, its deflationary nature and the increase in value make people believe in a better world again.

Of course, governments and especially the banking industry do not like it.

There are still many countries trying to abolish the BitCoin. In vain though. The threats are ultimately just a cry of despair.

This is where clarification is needed. The call for more regulation can be made, but if no one hears this call and implements it, it will fade away. The BitCoin cannot be regulated.

The FinTec industry has been devouring billions of dollars to invent their own "BitCoin", but all these projects have been plagued by technical limitations and mistakes. The most well known projects Ethereum and Ripple are hackable at any time and offer no security, yet the FinTec industry has high hopes for the systems.

The fact that Ethereum offers no security was recently proven on the Coinsbank Cruise.

The Satoshi School has made a decisive contribution to the importance of the BitCoin.

The ultimate goal is to guarantee people freedom in their decisions, unlimited payments and value creation or asset accumulation.

And this in a decentralized world, without paternalism and restrictions.

Those who understand BitCoins, the application of the Bit-Coin and the BitCoin Blockchain also understands why we need this world, why we do not need banks and government regulations.

The adaptation of the BitCoin and its increasing acceptance ensure that we can bring about political changes in a peaceful way.

The world is changing fundamentally. The BitCoin is able to change the world so that we get a basic income and a unified tax.

The EU and other countries are still fighting against it, they have recognised the BitCoin as a currency, but not as a substitute for today's currency not even as a reserve currency.

The EU wants to lift the anonymity by controlling and constantly monitoring all transactions. Just 5 million Euros have been made available for this, for the next 3 years. Interestingly, one notices that the politicians and all "experts" have no idea in the matter.

This year, a new technique for improving anonymity will be implemented. This makes all the work a waste of time, since the transactions are exchanged over several paths, with the same value from other transfers. Only senders and receivers therefore know about the transaction and can follow it in the Ledger, the public cashbook.

My school is there so that one can learn to position himself in this new world.

One thing will never change: Change in itself. And those who do not keep up with the time will disappear with the time.

At the time of writing, the BitCoin had a value of $ 2,800 and it continues to rise. In comparison, in 2006 it was at 465 US dollars.

114

People now have control over their own money.

Final thoughts

My sight sweeps unexpectedly towards the person sitting next to me's watch on the way to Paris. Nine thirty, 11.06.2017.

As I stare at his watch, I began to think. Can this be true? Is it really 9 years ago and Charlie Shrem is walking around free? It's as if all of this is a surreal fantasy that has been permanently implanted in the brain.

The world has definitely changed, but differently than expected.

The BitCoin is now established, causing pressure and anxiety for governments and banks. As a result, the Fin-Tec industry feels compelled to present new solutions of its own, ultimately resulting in empty ICO promises or dead-end alternative coins, such as pushing Ethereum and triggering hype, which is comparable with putting a Ferrari engine in a mummy.

Various MLM companies today claim to have invented new coins and outdo themselves with more and more insane ideas. A company then brought out the nonexistent One-Coin and the world was experiencing a new sect that even put Scientology in the shade. With blackmail and promises that didn't exist, millions of funds were retracted and misused.

Currently, BitCoin is being misused; big business is being done on people's ignorance.

On a daily basis, I am encouraged to continue expanding and promoting the Satoshi School.

At that time we took it for granted that you can only use something that really works and is not hollow based.

My life has changed fundamentally. There are not many people who understand BitCoin as a vision in itself. For the first time in history, we have the opportunity to lead people to a better world.

However, this requires education and a willingness to stop the FinTec industry more or less.

Basically, companies, governments, banks, etc. do not want decentralization. The idea that the citizen becomes competent causes them discomfort.

I look around New York on Wall Street, where people used to stand in the street and promote BitCoins. Today you don't see it anymore. The BitCoin has become a trading object and no longer a movement in the western world.

And other countries? We have to rethink, wake up to the fact that Japan, China, South Korea are much more advanced in dealing with BitCoins. Czech Republic, Poland, Ukraine are also further.

Here BitCoin are integrated in the public opinion. However a certain silence from Germany is commonplace. The Federal Financial Supervisory Authority (BaFin) issued a report saying BitCoin is a highly dangerous investment. Attitudes that are based on ignorance and fear. Those who compare BitCoin with PayPal are still among the most innocent unsuspecting.

We are now facing a mainstream breakthrough. More and more companies are coming onto the market, trying to capitalize on the increase in value of BitCoins by getting investors into a variety of models.

However, since investors can only pay in BitCoin, they must learn more about what it means to have Bit-Coins, leading sooner or later to questions and the Satoshi School can give answers.

As the keynote speaker at various events and being one of the "Top 100 Trainer Excellence" I can share the vision behind BitCoin.

Just like with this book.

With the feedback I have become, and my growing experience, confirms me to continue the mission. Nothing else would satisfy me.

I am often asked why I take the stress, instead of just taking the money and spend my life with travel and enjoy the beautiful sides of it.

Honestly, it pisses me off, this so-called "beautiful life." I went on land in Labadee (Haiti) to have a break from a cruise, where I spoke as a speaker.

This part of Haiti was created for tourists only. From there you cannot get inland. In a bay that takes an hour by foot, this is what you might call hell on earth.

The locals there have to react at the push of a button, as if in a zoo, exploited by and trying to sell their products of the mafia. These 'traders' are locked behind fences, where the stalls are. They cannot come directly on the street because that would be too annoying for tourists.

Considering that these people are doing even better than the others on the island, and then it is easy to guess what modern slavery is.

Above all, nobody really cares. Satiated, bloated... the passengers waddle down to the beach and spend a couple of hours lying on their towels before buying some souvenirs. At home raving about how great it was, the beach couldn't be any whiter. Disgusting!

But that's exactly where the vision starts. If it were possible to establish a constant educational program in each country, instead of being trapped behind fences, with the possibility to convert their own money into BitCoins, this would give them a real chance to afford education and other things, and secure a degree of independence.

Many donation funds can be fulfilled with BitCoins and the added value of leaving the money given, for one year, would make this way of funding projects a real blessing.

So I travel and carry on and teach people what the school and its vision can mean. And I know, in a few years, the world will be better than today. At least when dealing with money. Then the BitCoin will have almost completely replaced the traditional system and have largely destroyed debt policy, as well as people's dependence on it.

We will create a comprehensive educational network around the world. Governments and banks, with their own unsafe projects, will experience trickeries and hacker attacks and are forced to change to BitCoin. The dream of being able to separate the BitCoin from the Blockchain in the long run, is in for a rude awakening.

People want freedom, equal treatment and justice. There is no alternative to BitCoin, even if it is nicely promoted and packaged.

In this sense, I hope that you, dear reader, have been given an incentive and deciding push to position yourself. Because all the money you convert to BitCoin makes the price go up and ensures that everyone benefits from the added value, whether it's 20,000 in BitCoins or just 100. What matters is that people start to get rid of their previous dogmas. No matter how small the beginning may be. The world deserves it and so do you.

Scams and ICO's

When I started writing this book, the world was still pretty clear and there was the BitCoin world on one side and the FinTec industry's attempts to present their own solutions on the other side. If you like, it was a "battle" between the decentralized world (that's the one I stand for) and the centralized totalitarian surveillance demanded by governments and the financial sector.

Under the guise of terror, the argument is brought; the private person is in fact disestablished.

As you become more experienced in dealing with this world, you can quickly figure out where to start to make the world a better place to live. However, one forgets the potential that windy bookmakers have, the rip off artists, human traffickers and confidence tricksters.

There have been gigantic distribution channels around the BitCoin and all now claim that they have found the solution.

On a small scale, it looks like your best friend or someone you know calls you and says:

"I've got something, I have to show it to you. I can't tell you on the phone - YOU HAVE TO SEE IT."

As an old marketing expert in the call centre area, I would answer "... that must be a shit product, if you cannot even explain it on the phone :)".

120

You now make the cardinal mistake and let your friend / acquaintance explain more, and then full of himself he says "I will sell you everything now and you haven't a clue story." In addition, he promises you infinite commissions, a bonus plan, "... you have not seen something like that",...and kidnaps your brain into the bargain. In this multi-level marketing or almost snowball systems, you then run out there and sell something that does not exist.

None of these companies have a serious background and many of the names associated with them make you realise that quickly: all the windbags who then get rich, but the promise given "get out of the hamster wheel, too" and "live the way you want it" are promises of salvation for an army of poor sellers who have lost themselves at some point in an ideology of lies and self-sacrifice. Most of time they owe a favour to other "networkers".

And somehow the idea comes to a stop that these people are serious about having a "decentralized, free world" when they tell you, "You have to enrol more people, what's wrong with you".

A company pushed it so far that, although this company was banned in several countries and was not able to pay out, people are still asked to enrol.

The company One Coin, which then changed its name to One Life, has so far collected more than 400 million Euros in Germany, Austria and Switzerland, and no one knows where the money has gone.

They paid for their packages (up to 240,000 Euros).

These include so-called one-coins, which are better than the BitCoin and are also training packages.
And what happened now was something I never thought could be possible and yet the result is there:

A NEW SECT!

The training sessions are designed so that Ron L. Hubbard would turn around in the grave, why he did not think of it earlier. Since people have no idea about crypto-currency, these people first tell people to forget about BitCoin. They do that successfully. Many victims believe that BitCoin does not exist.

Add to that the indirect extortion factor. In order to achieve more sales, more and more is promised and nothing is held. At present you can only pay with One Coins in their own shopping system, where you additionally have to, strangely enough, pay the goods with Euros. Why is that then? The One Coin is just for people "without Coins". No value, then your back to the Euro. As simple as that.

And if you invested 240,000 today and someone locks your account, then you start to think.

But in order to keep the scam going, I have to prevent the victims from talking badly about the system. So it's good to find a way to get these people to sell more. So I tell them... "if you bring 100 new people, then there's money again".

Most people are so desperate that they start to find other victims. Greed rots your mind.

And above all, they do not allow criticism. The training is so good and the neuro linguistic programming short NLP works too. The people in this sect are considered to be a chosen community of enlightened beings who have sole knowledge and are only willing to pass it on if the new-comer "openly and impartially accepts the teachings".

Every MLM turbo seller dreams of sales figures that the One Coin sect has achieved.

Therefore, the most curious inventions can be found again: Ducatus Coin, Platinum Coin, Pura (or formerly Pura Vida) and so on.

Some companies are taking other paths. So the company Avalon, which promises a new world vision and has its own coin, the Pura. An illusion that persisted for a long time and you can buy land in Costa Rica, get returns for emission rights, participate in a Crypto village and as the whole thing blew up, thanks to my research, there now is a project for pure water.

And so the MLM always reinvents themselves. Old game, new packaging. Fast money lures and it is there too, but then comes the gambling addiction and the money is lost as quickly as acquired.

The truth always comes to light, for some, however, only when they have already lost everything, without realising it.

Life is like a large brothel and many are lost in its corri-dors. A labyrinth of consumer terror, greed and delusion in which the Beelzebub and the cat spit and laugh back a thousand times at the stupid victims of the marketing machinery as they fold the notes listening to hip music then building the next corridors.

As an atheist with Buddhist views (the philosophical part of Buddhism), one is resistant to any kind of "believe it, then it becomes real, and we have that, and we will,... etc.".

Why do people always want to conjure up something and not take the BitCoin in social networking?

Well, real decentralized currency cannot make money. The BitCoin is too honest. You cannot fake your cash-book, you can't say that something that does not exist, has a growing value. So if you are not able to buy BTC yourself or make your own, you have to try to get some other product. And then there are all the promises to get the BitCoins out of your pocket.

If you bought 10 BitCoins worth 4,650 Euros in March 2016, they are now worth 25,000 Euros. Such an increase you wouldn't get anywhere, and that will go on until 2140, only then will the last BitCoin see the light of day.

I founded the project "Satoshi School Scam Cam" in June 2017 and report daily about the scene of the "Honourable Society", which only wants "your best", your hard-earned BitCoins. Here, these fraudsters are also called by name and exposed.

Because everyone knows:

In five years the BitCoin will have reached the 10,000

Euro mark.

As a means of payment BitCoins is currently increasing globally. More and more merchants are accepting BitCoins.

There is a distribution battle going on right now. Of the 16.8 million only 6.5 million BitCoins are in circulation, that said, the price must rise. In addition, the output of new BitCoins is halved approximately every four years, and new ones will never be printed again when the maximum number of 21,000,000 BTCs has been created.

The FinTec industry invested $ 45 billion in the development of Blockchains and own coins in 2015-2016, and no system is safe or operating properly.

And now, all over the place, new ones are coming in and everyone has a secure Blockchain with its own coin. Strange only with their super techniques, they cannot sell to the banks thus collecting a lot more money, which then the people from the MLM would profit from...

The FinTec industry came up with a new scam of collecting money:

ICO - Initial Coin Offering

Short and sweet are such terms, yes, always some hip and "up to date", but the name behind it is confusing and not suitable for the layman to understand. But I'll release you from the guesswork and explain briefly what an ICO is.

In the age of digitization, stock trading with paper is already antiquated and thus not particularly exciting. In addition, the deposits at the banks are also in digital form. Further development now looks like this:

FinTec announces a new project:

There is a description, and because at the moment everyone wants to be first, millions are being collected. Recently, a company managed to collect 120 million in 3 hours with their idea. In return, you get a stake in the company. This is given out as digital proof, which is held in the Blockchain (tokens). This digital share can then be traded on exchanges.

The problem:

Of all the companies that have launched an ICO in the last 2 years, just 20 percent have launched a product. More and more people are wasting money in these ICs and they do not know what they are doing.

The FinTec industry is not unhappy that money invested is being misused, the so called ‚digital enslavement‘ carries on and the enthusiasm stays because no one understands the real effect of what's going on.

This has nothing to do with painting everything black, but with human nature. There are leaders and followers, as in the animal world. And the alpha leader needs money to show how much power he can command. It is not about who has little or a lot of money but the individual who has more money feels more reassured and self-important.

126

As a result, he will think more and more how to get people to underpin his supremacy with more money. As you can see in the story of some state leaders today, logic can be replaced by money-based power.

And now a vast network of information is being set up, which will be a financial strait jacket for people who will lose freedom over their money. The spreading of "pleasant" news, which will guarantee peace of mind. Total control.

And that's why I can't say enough... be self-reliant and self-confident.

The Satoshi School has therefore created several options:

- Comprehensive training in handling and using the digital currency

- Clarification on the legal situation and legality, BitCoin and the changes, and why no bank is able to shut down or control the system and never will

- Demonstrate opportunities in private wealth assets and back up with BitCoin

Those who do not keep up with the time, will go with the time.

In a new world you have to find your way around, for that you need a compass and courage to accept something new. I will make sure your path does not end in a blind alley.

Anonymity in the BitCoin world

Fact or wishful thinking?

The BitCoin Blockchain is until now the only Blockchain that was not hacked or otherwise faked.

Due to the importance of the BitCoin for freedom, self-determination and a symbol of peace, to escape surveillance and to free oneself from the countries tampering, the question arises, how anonymous am I in this BitCoin world?

First of all, let's look at the moral side: Do I have to be anonymous, where there are so many black sheep?

This first needs a definition of what black sheep are.

Our society, in which we live freely, as an example Germany enables us to find ourselves in many groups of like-minded people, thus defining in the group itself what is morally acceptable to us, where our definition of freedom begins, and where it ends, depending on what your view of the world is, and that can vary quite a bit. That's why it's not bad or negative to be in the BitCoin world, because everyone is equal.

I'll give you an example:

You are a drug lord and you have some girls working for you. You make a lot of money by raising addicts and the prostitutes who work for you. In order to get your money

128

safe, you choose to buy BitCoins.

Now you do not just buy for 1,000 Euros, but regularly for 50,000 Euros. So you are narrowing the amount offered and you are indirectly raising the price of the BitCoin. The one who now voluntarily buys drugs at a market place that you have created is ultimately responsible for himself and the state can not play daddy for him. This is the same boy who stole the credit card from the father and gets money out of the ATM and buys drugs at the corner.

Your girls, you exploit, now hear randomly from our saving plan model, which from 01.08. - 01.10. when ICO is launched (www.bitcoin-pension.com).

Now, with the little money they have, they convert 5 percent each month into BitCoins. In five years, the price of BTC is at 30,000 and rising until 2140. In five years these people will be able to free themselves from your extortionate ways, and with a small amount they can build up a fortune. By having learned to be careful with money, they will invest the money relatively quickly and meaningfully.

So that means, ultimately, because you have money invested in BitCoins, you've done good things for the world that exists at lower levels, even if you do not want to. In the broader sense, you even contribute to the fact that the government system must eventually commit itself to basic income and a unitary tax.

From this example you can see that ethical ideas play no role for BitCoin.

In order for this to work, we also need to get the ones

that are living at a lower level into BitCoins.

That is the task, not only for me, and the school, but for everybody. This is a joint project to create a better future. We cannot prevent evils from existing, but we will help make the world fair, and above all, that people can act again with self-determination. In freedom, no matter who suppresses them, because money is the means by which we can free ourselves.

However, in order for us to be able to live our lives independently, we need a protective function, and that means anonymity.

UNFORTUNATLY, PEOPLE DON'T PROTECT THEIR OWN ANONYMITY.

That's the problem. We live in a time where we voluntarily disclose our data at any time. Let's take the example of multi-level marketing, MLM for short.

Many people expect a new life in financial freedom, through passive income. Such a system presupposes that more and more people are joining into the system where the money is then redistributed amongst the higher levels.

This is the way many people try to get to BitCoins, because normally you can only buy yourself into the system with BitCoins. That's because the founders of these networks know that BitCoins prices are going to explode in a couple of years and of course they want to own as many BitCoins as possible.

130

With these systems, when you log in, you have to do some KYC, but always specify your own data.

Surprisingly, it does not bother anyone that he is not getting the data from the operators, place of residence, etc.

So now everyone knows what you are doing with your BitCoins. Even better is the fact that the operator of such MLM also earns by reselling the address data, including e-mails, also to authorities.

We get credit cards that are BTC based and we are, as in the old world, completely traceable. I don't particularly care, but there are people who want to stay anonymous.

So the EU is starting to build huge databases with the help of the NSA, where who did what, when and at what time, and where it appeared in connection with BitCoins.

So it does not help at all if such great techniques start like TumbleBit and Mimblewimble, when you are responsible for being linked by investigators.

Also, you are evidently linked to the stock exchanges and known by name.

So it's up to you to protect yourself.

What options do I have?

When you have your money converted into BItCoins, you have to leave the exchange or stock exchange and distribute your BitCoins to other wallets.

Use a VPN for example: VPN.ht

Warn users against Xapo, Coinbase, and Bitpanda, because they are a well known victim of government requests, etc. By all three of them have already accounts being closed arbitrary.

Never share your information with strangers. Only go into those networks that offer you anonymity, such as BCN. If the ponzi system dies off, it is better to accept a loss than an additional loss of your own data. Buy at localbitcoins.com.

Register under a foreign name. Find someone who does the KYC for you.

Spread your coins on several wallets.

In fact, it is still possible to move anonymously, through TumbleBit, Breezewallets, Mimblewimble and Dandelion we are protected in the network and on getting there.

If you use BitCoins BitSquare or Paxful to buy BitCoin, you remain anonymous and can even buy with Sepa BTC without the bank being able to track you.

I think, it is always up to you to protect yourself from harm.

Taxes

Please note the following: There is a lot being said about taxes in the BitCoin field, and there are many questions that tax advisors still not answer properly. Get a picture of it yourself.

132

This is not tax advice, but material compiled in the form of journalistic research.
A tax advisor you trust should always draw up a proper tax declaration, and he should obtain information about the current situation.

General introduction

In 2008, Satoshi Nakamoto introduced a new digital currency and opened it to the public. Over the past 8 years, the currency has been accepted globally, and there are numerous regulations on how to deal with the taxation of this crypto currency.

With a present value of $ 1,600 at the time of writing, Bit-Coin is at a very high level due to its decentralized nature and the lack of government and monetary institutions, such as a central bank or other issuing offices.

The currency lives especially from the absence of third parties, the computer algorithm and the underlying protocol takes over this task.

The system cannot be hacked due to its encryption technology and has been running stable since 2008.

Quantity limitation and the halving of the amount every 4 years ensure that the BitCoin is deflationary.

Looking at BitCoin as a currency, as defined by the EU, Germany took a different approach and thus the tax considerations do not differ in terms of lexus, but in lex specialis from European and national law.

There are now some counselling centres that rely on this complex matter of taxation, but usually follow the wrong paths.

This book is intended to provide an overview of how to look at tax approaches.

We endeavour to keep this work up to date, but point out that this is not a formal tax advice. Please speak to a trusted tax advisor.

Outline of the problem

Probably the biggest challenge is the fact that the BitCoin is not controlled by anyone, but people are able to use this freely and the transaction directory is led not by name, but encrypted numbers. Moreover, the transactions are mixed according to the principle that the recipient is not interested in the picture on the 1 Euro coin, but only the value "1 Euro".

Thus, a following of transactions by sender and receiver is impossible. Ultimately, taxation will therefore only be based on voluntary information provided by the person willing to pay.

However, proper taxation also has various advantages.

Previous development in the area of taxes and law

The European Union has classified BitCoin as a currency. Regulations within the EU deviate from German law.

Under American law, a BitCoin license is required to aut-
horize trading and exchange with BitCoins.
The core problem in American law, based on the BitCoin
License, is the fact that credit in BitCoins must be in stock
as a Fiat currency.

Since this is an unmet need for 90 percent of the trading
venues and exchanges, many BitCoin companies are no
longer active in the US. Coin base, for example, has with-
drawn from all countries that have adopted US law, most
recently from Hawaii.

After initial attempts in China to use control measures
(death penalty) and Russia, the BitCoin was legalized and
recognized there, Russia sees it as a cash flow, but a fi-
i
nal decision as currency recognition by the DUMA is still
pending. On the page https://coin.dance/poli the current
classification of BitCoins can be viewed worldwide.

Classification of the BTC European law /
German-speaking area

Legislation BaFin

Due to the European Union's classification that the Bit-
Coin is exempt from VAT, it was subsequently recognized
as a means of payment in the form of its own currency.

The German Federal Government, represented by the
Minister of Finance Schäuble, vehemently rejects this
classification and as a result BitFin is treated as a private
means of payment by the BaFin and defined as a currency

in accordance with the German Banking Act.

Special tax problems

Due to its classification as a currency, acting as an agent with commission to exchange Euros in BitCoins is not permitted in Germany and requires a special permit according to §34.

Example:

Someone gives you 5,000 Euros and you exchange them into BitCoins and transfer them to the remitter. For that you receive a certain amount of money. Then this is an activity in the placing of assets that you cannot do without a special permit. See also section 1 (11) of the Banking Act.

The basic problem with this is that the BitCoin cannot act as a foreign exchange at all:

Subsuming the BitCoin under the facts of the definition of a currency:

1) A calculable unit

All currencies are so-called calculable units. For example, the euro was based on a calculable unit following its introduction in order to facilitate the exchange of DM into Euros. This calculable unit also underlies the switch between the euro and the Swiss franc, after the latter decided to leave the monetary union.

136

That is, a fixed issue price is set.

2) Issuing central bank

The value and the expenditure of these calculable units are strictly dependent on the central banks of the respective country.

To 1) The BitCoin is not a foreign exchange because its value depends on supply and demand as well as existing value of goods.

To 2) The BitCoin has no central bank. The participants in the payment transaction keep a single, decentralized, digital cashbook, which is not forfeitable and where the entries are automatically generated by protocol as soon as a transaction has gone through the elaborate, secure examination procedure and are recognized as being valid.

Conclusion: a tax assessment is objectively and mathematically wrong and thus any tax assessment is contestable until a general binding statutory regulation by the government occurs.

Thus, ultimately, all tax assessments based on the above-mentioned assumption of BaFin pending are ineffective, since there is no alternative legal regulation.

Furthermore, here is a violation with the EU. EU law applies as a general rule before German law.

Thus, the BitCoin is to be understood as a currency and a private exchange of currencies (as long as it has no business intention, so advance payment and commissi-on-free) is not prohibited.

The process described above would be completely legal.

Questions

The word crypto currency is wrong. Many crypto curren-cies have no ideal or material value, but only a specula-tive, marketable value, which is not measured on com-modities, etc., has no current assets (about 790 of 800 currencies). Thus, a tax perspective can only refer to the BitCoin, which is named as such and on which everything is measured. The BitCoin is a digital currency and in the actual E-Money, a similant to PayPal. The denial of BTC as e-money is currently a social consensus.

2) By law, all accounts at exchanges and banks worldwide are reporting to the BaFin, so it is at least possible that by the exchanges the tax offices make inquiries and respond accordingly.

3) On the basis of honest taxation of the income, one can proceed as follows:

A) Maintain an entry and exit book via BitCoin payments

B) Adhere to the intended use.

C) Information about the sender of the money does not apply, since here privacy rights are respected, which can-not be repealed by law.

D) The amount of income that is taxable can therefore
138

be measured after the profit and loss is calculated. That is, what was the price at time X of the payment made or when the incoming payment actually happened?

E) The BitCoins achieved through mining, purchase of an exchange or from the profit generated through commodity trading, etc. also by taxes for fixed and passive assets. The value is then taxed once and added to the balance. This can certainly lead to an increase in company assets.

F) Taxation and its importance - if the BitCoin was used as a means of payment or as a means of exchange, for example, property value against BitCoin. As a rule, BitCoin payments are converted via a credit card and then the payment process is initiated. It should be noted that it is exempt from VAT. On the other hand, if I accept a bit coin directly and sell goods that were not in the current assets of the Euro, this is a barter transaction and I am completely tax-exempt.

G) BitCoin output and acceptance in BitCoins: The Bitcoin is in a closed circuit. If goods from own production (which were not previously in the Fiat circulation) and services are offered, the BitCoin is not taxable, since there is no regulation in the BitCoin world for tax control. There is also no intersection with the Fiat money. That would therefore be only a voluntary commitment to tax payment (for example via a DAO consensus).

H) BitCoins from trading and trading networks generally have a one-year waiting period, and this is verifiable on the stock exchange where they are acquired. So you cannot move them, from there, to your own wallet. The time of acquisition must be proven and also the whereabouts of the BitCoins. The hash code is therefore written down and verified by means of account statements.

I) No taxation, the sales price depends on supply and demand, BitCoin is exempt from VAT. Exception: An additional charge is generated on the average stock market value, e.g. Selling via Local BitCoins. In Germany this corresponds to a foreign exchange trading with profit intention and is not permitted without a §34c note. If such a note is present, the profit is taxable and the BitCoin as such is then subject to foreign exchange trading. It should be noted that taxation may be subject to international exchange laws and thus may incur premiums from Lombard's interest business. Basically, the seller is obliged to taxation, so that, for example, stock exchanges generally bear the tax burden.

J) Mining - If I can prove that I own properties on my own computers, whether at home or the mining pool, the creator principle applies. The BitCoins are completely tax-free even after the sale. It's as if the farmer takes out a potato from the ground. The value of the potato comes about only through the sale. It is the same with the BitCoin. Mining is not a profit generation, but equates to new currencies from the central. Because we life with the principle of proof, the financial tax authorities must in the case of disputing the credibility of the statement „the BitCoins come from mining with their own makings" bring proof.

K) If I buy hardware shares, etc., whether by credit card or BTC, I am not taxable, but the recipient of the money is because he sold hardware and administration services, and is thus subject to the income tax.

L) However, if dividend payouts are made out of commissions, whether domestically or abroad, regardless of whether they are paid in BTC or another currency, they must be fully taxed. In case of doubt, the financial authorities will tax all receipts from non-definable, non-accountable companies. The taxpayer is obliged to show proof of invoice.

M) NetWork Marketing revenues billed as commissions are fully taxable.

In the case of regular buying and selling (trading), a commercial operation is generally assumed, unless it can be proven that no personal enrichment has taken place (recording of all stock market values at the time of the sale, that is, the price the sale may not exceed the purchase value you yourself had. The European guidelines are Xapo and Bitstamp. Everything on top of that is understood as a business sense. If the purchase price is below the selling price, a differential taxation is the result. If you can prove that the profits from Trading have been resting for a year, they will be tax-free.

Taxation in accordance with the corporate tax law, you can expect profit taxation from trading or investment of trader monies, etc.

If mining is used solely for itself and the sale of BTC is made on your own account, the producer clause will apply and no taxation will result. This is, as I said, only for BTC mining, everything that has also been described, not to be confused with AltCoin Mining.

If the company sells shares in mining, the purchases of

such shares are taxable.

The imports of BitCoins to Germany are then foreign currency and are subject to the law on the taxation of foreign currency.

Taxation also applies whenever the BTC is directly related to the trade/business.

As long as the BTC is on your own account, no tax. The question of origin always arises from the Inland Revenue. Also if it doesn't come from mining. Even if someone gave me a BTC or if I traded goods that are new and do not come from the Fiat world there is no tax to be paid. In the case where I withdraw goods from the Fiat system, taxes have to flow; otherwise I would damage the system in terms of value.

LG makes a TV and doesn't sell it on its traditional distribution channels, but directly to you for BTC. Then LG does not need to show its transaction.

If the dealer at Media Markt takes an LG TV from his stock and sells it for BTC, he has to pay tax on this income, i.e. the value of the BTC.

The employer transfers your salary to a bank and pays you in BitCoins. Since you get your net salary (thus the salary after deduction of taxes), this is tax-free (otherwise there would be double taxation).

The BTC is exempt from VAT. The recipient of the money must pay taxes.

Loss / profit can lead to a price deviation, if one accepts in BTC. On the other hand, there is instant payment. Suppliers pay directly in Euros at the same time as payment is met, so no exchange risk.

In the case of BTC being received directly, the fluctuation in value is to be taken into consideration when doing tax returns. Thus itemisation, which BitCoin was accepted, at which price?

The easiest way to pay taxes is to create your own account statement in Euros at the relevant rate and specify the purpose of use only. Then go to the tax consultant and calculate what your tax-load will be. Sell BTC to the amount of the tax burden on the exchange and done.

If the BTC is banned in Germany, then you have a problem. You are not allowed to use the BTC anymore. Furthermore, one is known by name to the exchanges, that one holds a BTC account. In other words, if you have not spent your BTC elsewhere, the account may be suspended as a result. Especially with exchanges and trading platforms, as has already happened with Xapo.

BitCoins are legal. And therefore the exchanges including the exchange or sale on LocalBitCoins etc.

In the event that BTC accounts are visible and you have BitCoins there (i.e. Xapo as exchange, the GV on the BaFin can see it), it can be seized. Foreign exchange is after all just fixed assets. If you have not stated that you could face prison.

Monetary assets as a currency. However, if I take my private keys to the grave, an implementation of the claims is no longer possible.

The world is upside down

Today a call from the bank, the legal department. During my whole life I have never been called by the banks legal department and yes, it makes me feel a bit edgy!

"We want to talk to you about your last transaction, waiting here to be finalised."

The first question that came to me is why the legal department? What have I done wrong? A transfer to another bank, even though I want to deposit clean, honest money somewhere else, or just wanting to buy something. Not even that, me wanting to exchange my money for another currency?

Perplexity.

The man or the woman on the phone continues "...You have made a mistake. Your money is not safe where you transferred it. You have to expect a total loss!"

I'm confused. I wonder what this call is all about. Does this person not know the laws?

I ask, "How long have you been doing your job? Do you think such calls will save your job, or is it more that you make me change my bank and only live from BitCoins?"

Silence at the other end. Then the following statement: "Anyone who supports a criminal system and opposes an

144

established system of reason and trust, cannot expect serious support!"

I reply, "You have described your bank very aptly, Bit-Coins are fortunately incorruptible."
A bitter aftertaste remained after I hung up. Will they still do the transfer?

The transfer was made. It would not be possible to refuse. Currency is still currency and therefore I am untouchable. At the moment!

What we see here is the Bank's realisation that it faces an imminent exodus of existence and cannot stop it.

Regulation, misinformation and the press sounding the alarm bells will not bring BitCoin to its knees.

BitCoin users across the EU are at record levels, and now in Austria it is possible to buy BitCoins in every post office or in Switzerland at every station.

The biggest social experiment in history shows that society is still, or, thank God, living and being aware that things cannot go on like this.

Without the electoral fraud, LePenn would probably have brought down the EURO.

The world votes right in protest against a substantiation of a digital enslavement. Man as a freethinker and creator is de facto abolished by law and perceived as a terrorist threat.

Tax evasion, which have existed since the invention of money, as a means of exchange, is stylized to such an extent that it is necessary to doubt the claimant's mental attitude.

In general terms, we are badly off people threatened by everything and everyone. Especially by Hartz IV, TV depriving people of an individual existence. Conspirators and regimes accuse each other of wrongdoing, and the truth, if there is one at all, disappears in the eyes of the victims, who simply want to be objectively informed.

The cleric is today also only a concubine of abuse using the name of Allah, God or someone else. Faith moves mountains and makes our mind blind.

And now here comes the BitCoin. Its system allows only the pure truth, because it is an unchanging world diary. Once entered, an event can no longer be changed. A timestamp for eternity.

I can manipulate the odometer of a car, but if the original value remains in place in the BitCoin Blockchain Ledger, the offender can be caught.

But everyone is afraid of a world in which truth is no longer just a trick but a means of control for those who want to control us.

And so the fine gentlemen who called us today and enlightened us that we are doing wrong, fall victim in their own cauldron.

And that's good. Because independence means decentralisation.

With this in mind, I wish you much pleasure with your BitCoins. Treat each one well, because it is your ticket to freedom.

2018 - The final battle to the territory of the money management has begun

One day you will probably recite these lines as a time testimony, because in the world of BitCoin there is not just logic, but a lot of misunderstanding and misinterpretation.

The best way to recognize look for Bitcoin enthusiasts and Blockchain hardliners. On the other hand, the Bitcoin users, who says the end of the banks and of the whole of society, and all of them is the change, are the BitCoin users, who take on the balls cheerfully, while the FinTec industry takes up the rhetoric of the governments and central banks and makes mood against the BitCoin Institutions, come see.

In the meantime, BitCoin has had to multiply hard forks and the resulting BitCoin Cash (affectionately called BCrash or BCash) has become a symbol for investors becoming greedy for money and megalomaniac.

A few weeks ago (in April 2018) the dispute over the "true" BitCoin escalated. Actually, the question would not arise at all, since when Community BCash was generated, it was decided that BitCoin (BTC) would remain the only one and true, while BCash (BCH) loses and jumped to the AltCoin league. BCash has to assert itself there.

But as it is with the eternal second, who do not realize that their chance is past. You fight for the last straw: generate attention with the crowbar.

There are the scandals about the misleading of the name BitCoin. The BitCoin specialist blog of Roger Ver has begun to coronation to change the phrase in the articles. It is now called more Bitcoin (BCH) and if it is reported on the real BitCoin, this is then called Bitcoin Core. Even a court case leads to the whole thing now.

Before that there was an attempt to change and rewrite the whitepaper, the "holy grail" of the BitCoin followers.

It's no longer a question of whether a network with larger blocks is better than a network with SegWit and Lightning.

Here, too, BCH is now beaten off. The Lightning network now has more nodes and more transactions than BCash. Since then BCash has been trying to keep his community happy with crazy projects.

It is not difficult to see what is true and what is wrong. Finally, behind BCash stands a company called NChain, which has given, among others, the wrong Satoshi Nakamoto, Steven Craig Wright, a home. The one Gavin Andresen is convinced he really is Satoshi Nakamoto (and other prominent supporters see it that way). This "fake" Satoshi Nakamoto, who gets stuck in a lawsuit for allegedly ripping off his partner.

So does that look like finding a truth or a coin that believes it has more acceptance than Bitcoin?

Further developments for the Bitcoin - Lightning

In the next few weeks, the long-awaited Lighning network with its own wallets for the masses will finally be launched. This nodal system is supported by the traditional Bitcoin network. Simply put, on request the transactions go to the Lightning network. In this case, the signature of a transaction is separated from the code by SegWit.

While Lightning is processing the transaction, only those signatures are used in Lightning's network. Thus, a theft of transactions is impossible, because only with the complete transaction, which persists in the Bitcoin network until the security and arrival of the signature at the receiver is guaranteed, the entry can be made in the ledger.

Then the transaction is entered in the public directory and declared valid.

Should anything go wrong during the execution phase, the signature will be attached to its original transaction and the miners will then process it using the traditional Bitcoin method.

In this way, Lightning has the ability to execute up to 1 million transactions per second via the so-called Paychannel, which are deeply anchored with the BitCoin Blockchain.

The business to business field (B2B) can now also be served by BitCoin.

Regulators and FinTec - The Empire is attacking - out of ignorance and the fear of it

Be it the so-called Private Coins (created for invisible transactions) which are to be banished from the stock exchanges, starting in Japan, or in India all exchanges may no longer make any change between fiat money and digital currencies, the list of blows against Bitcoin are getting curious.

In numerous conferences, from the Coinsbank Cruise to the Miami Blockchain Nation, the Global Blockchain Conference and the World Blockchain and Crypto Summit in Moscow, to such crucial conferences as Finopolis, the picture is the same everywhere:

Fear on the part of governments and banks. Lies and even more lies by central banks and the shopkeepers from the ICO industry, which would have learned nothing but hot air and the much-loved "if, could, would" - phrases.

In the second year of the ICO boom, lunatic fairy tales are dangled into a possible blockchain, so that every human being who can still think normally thinks about the head. Far more than 500 million dollars have already been sacked and countless opportunities and funds have been lost. Money that would have made the BitCoin Blockchain the safest instrument for protecting property and the unchangeability of smart contracts, and today would all actually live in a better, more peaceful and honest financial environment.

But truth is not the world in which people want to live. If you turn the speedometer of a car back to indulge in greed or simply out of financial hopelessness, you can not fraud the data written in the BitCoin Blockchain, about the right mileage.

But who wants that? Who wants to live in a world where truth as good is protected from hostile attacks, through deception, glare and loss of reality.

All blockchain projects and altcoins serve only two things:

Control and profit maximization.

One only has to listen to the preachers of this new block-chain world, as they occupy their central databases with the name Blockchain and thus draw millions by misleading.

Is it any wonder that the regulators strike and central banks, "in the chorus of yesteryear", sing the song of the old sea, then pay homage to Neptune in the Shanty, before the whole show sinks.

The smell of decay is in the air, but the vindication of traditional rhetorician's clings to the abyss of philosophy, in a shadowy existence, until the light of knowledge finally brings them to collapse. An earthquake of such magnitude as to drive the global economy and the financial world to an unprecedented catastrophe.

It will be in the history books read: "The end of the financial world was sealed after the years of tug-of-war for new systems finally took its toll and the few who saw this now evolved to the new money managers this earth, because the BitCoin price in the millions lap. Ignorance and know-it-all, demonization and clinging to old paradigms have already been the downfall of many objectors, such as Nokia. Those who do not learn from the past are doomed to relive them over and over again."

Mark Zuckerberg said in 2018, "... he is truly sorry that this data scandal has arisen ..." and he will do everything so that such an event does not repeat itself.

Only the damage is great. Now people are finally transparent to every businessman, every advertising company, every government, everything. The company, which has received the data from almost all its members (about 2 billion), will now be carrying out large-scale analysis and making available to all those who find a connection and can misuse it for their own purposes.

And there will also be apologies, from giant blockchain projects that have "accidentally" lost control of ownership and purpose, and now have to justify the ownership of millions of people who have been hacked and brought over their property. People mistakenly lost their homes, cars stopped charging, service providers stopped receiving goods, and the payment system collapsed. Huge amounts of security-relevant data falls to terrorists, who have been waiting for a new opportunity, secured the assumption of rights to the national water and electricity supply. The digital identities have been destroyed and millions of people have been excluded from the system overnight and de facto homeless and stateless.

2018 is the year in which the final battle for property, payment transactions and the design of digital contracts has begun

The race of humanity, against total surveillance and digital enslavement.

Will George Orwell 1984, Enemy of the state #1, Mocking-jay, Maze Runner, etc., be right and people go to their own destruction, controlled by a few in a powerful computer network that will ultimately lose control?

The work of the Satoshi School and Vision begins where others have long since given up what to move. Become part of a vision that redirects the world to self-determination and puts totalitarian surveillance in its place. Become master of your data and your life again. It is time!

Enlightenment gives everyone involved a chance to find themselves in a world of constant change. In a world that redefines itself and creates with it new rules of coexistence, economy and government. Driven by consensus, monitored by an independent computer network.

The BitCoin Blockchain! The surest answer to the question of self-determination and digital protection against access by third parties at the present time, without having to trust people.

The BitCoin

Fascination? Nightmare? Both?

"The BitCoin came to stay" is a popular quote that is used more and more often today. Others say, "BitCoin will eventually be replaced by another digital currency, because it's only the beginning, and as with many beginnings, the true potential of a digital currency will come later."

The whole idea has only one catch. You cannot just see the BitCoin as a means of payment or a value transfer system. You cannot disassociate the BitCoin from the Bit-Coin Blockchain.

All attempts to do so sooner or later have failed. Not least by BC Cash.

All so-called AltCoins are hackable, except for those who have copied the BitCoin Blockchain system 1:1.

No one has ever managed to create a secure system. Etherum, Ripple and most recently the EOS project have weaknesses.

The FinTec industry said: "It took us 2 years to understand the BitCoin and the BitCoin Blockchain. Now we are finally able to build our own systems."

The consequence, hacked wallets, stock exchanges, DAO

and it will go on, recently many ICO projects were robbed, where not all came out in public to protect Ethereum.
The FinTec industry set up reserves to protect against a
possible price slump with fresh capital in order to ensure
"investment security".

You see, the old economy system, with the same mistakes, "goes digital". Blockchain is today a well-known
term, a common term. Where it is written Blockchain it
does not have to have a block-chain in it, and it's gushing
up the money.

Recently, the R3 consortium presented us with Allianz
insurance. We take a couple of servers, a few clusters,
do it three times (example: insurance -> registration /
customer -> insurance / insurance -> insurance (request
damage)

We call the whole thing Blockchain and "a coin" or "we do
not need a special backup, we trust ourselves, and these
are private chains". Payments are only taken in cash "and
hopefully I will not experience the day where we have to
allow BitCoins" (Direct quote from the Allianz insurance at
Ethereum Meetup in Munich).

What happens then will be the following: After everything
has taken a few years, you realise that you don't really
need that, better to reduce the servers, and then we're
back to the old system with just a new name.

The question I asked, "why is it called a BlockChain when
it's not that at all?" The following answer came "How much
advertising do you want to do, in order that people understand the difference? Ask somebody about a Kleenex

Tissue, because in the end you do not care what you get, it just has to fulfil its function".

FAITH IN BLOCKCHAINS AND COINS HAVE ALREADY RUINED SOME.

The difference for the BitCoin is, I can spend the BitCoin somewhere in a store, I can send it to friends on Twitter, Wallets, etc. I can use credit cards as an interface for Fiat / BitCoin and BitCoin / Fiat.

Probably the most fantastic product exhibit is seen at the company mobi.me, which has just launched a mobile wallet and with which I can spend my BitCoins in all countries in the world at the lowest fees. In the app I can exchange BitCoins in all currencies that exist, in both directions.

I can decide if I want to send BitCoins to a colleague who owns this app, or the respective currency. In ten minutes, he has the money, no matter where he is in the world and the fees are almost non-existent, compared to conventional methods.

Anyone who has ever travelled around the world with this app knows how great that is.

Basically, that would be the perfect combination of both worlds. But do we want that? Yes and no. The "YES" is clearly based on usability. Also the handling.

On the other hand, it is another step away from the independence the BitCoin has created. We depend on a third party for convenience.

Many Europeans are therefore easily ensnared to see the BitCoin only from an economic point of view. Leave it and let it increase in value, trade with it.

The BitCoin itself was once invented as a means of payment to give guest workers the ability to send money home without high fees.

Over the years, the asset class has repeatedly sought to bring volatility under control.

"The BitCoin must be subject to strict, stable regulation in order to provide security for investors," is the unanimous call from banks and governments.

"Any kind of abuse and impassability due to an unpredictable amount of users can not be the goal of an economically controlled industry that wants government protection for consumers."

These phrases are heard over and over again and so it finally led in the US to the introduction of KYC and the BitLicense.

If you look closely, it is a paradox ad absurdum!

We want to counteract a controlled power-obsessed money system that experienced a near collapse in 2008, with our own free currency, and now we are pleading to those who brought the system to its knees, to give us rules.

The Winklevoss brothers, Roger Ver and other characters from earlier times, are unlike me, driven by the idea of achieving maximum output with little input.

The discussion about ETF or non-ETF is just the tip of the iceberg and that it was rejected is in my opinion the first time ever that something was done for the BitCoin and not against it.

REAL VALUE OF THE BITCOIN VS. BUBBLE SPECULATION

Through the ETF, tensions were at a peak; price fluctuations witnessed do no justice to the BitCoin. The BitCoin price will be unpredictable and many people would be plunged into misery.

The banking crisis has shown us where it leads too when we rely on bear raiding, price betting, etc., and turning values into other assets causing a circle of debt. Ultimately, you could then bet on payment default, ‚credit protection'.

Greed for money is not just "a" greed. Joe Madisson once said, "It's the passion of collecting. Money that cannot be spent anymore because of the amount of it, is then not an asset, but it is a passion of collecting".

We have already learned this from the funny paperbacks with Uncle Dagobert. The good-natured Donald and his clever nephews live in modest circumstances, which Uncle Dagobert disregards, but just in case, he will go through the greatest adventure, to increase his money even more, sometimes with fabulous tricks.

He guards every taller like a treasure, spending it makes him feel painful.

And yet, Uncle Dagobert is the perfect reflection of a society whose desire for the object of money is insatiable. Uniqueness, that cannot be achieved, makes people spend millions.

The bought up image. Entire industries thrive on selling over-priced goods, but these are only available in limited quantities to underpin the "exclusive status".

It can't be just one Dalmatian, nope 101 Dalmatians. Business and greed go before morality. We preach decentralization and lure people into dependence on structural systems that put us in a dependency. Where the structural boss acts as if he were the king and the others his lackeys.

The BitCoin has a complete other basis.

The BitCoin will always be only partially an investment and a controllable value system.

On the other hand, it is alive, does not abide by social standards and breaks with all the rules again and again, and can't be stopped.

What many considered a bad joke today is nearly $ 3,500 worth per BitCoin.

Hardly anyone can explain the ups and downs. It behaves in an opposing way and then presents conformity for a while.

At this very moment, it makes its political component visible.

160

THE REAL VALUE

The real value of BitCoin is the non-speculative side of BitCoin.

The Fiat character of BitCoin, as an unrivalled, unique, not manipulability world currency (Wright had placed the term 'centrally' rather than unrivalled at this point and was subsequently given a Shit Storm) cannot be refuted.

The rise in price of BitCoin comes from supply and demand, but unlike AltCoins, there are two different components here:

- Demand due to trading volumes at stock exchanges and financial service providers (speculative bubble)

- Demand due to need from life situations (real value demand)

The real-value demand ensures that the BitCoin remains in circulation and at the same time has a currency function, with which we buy groceries and everyday things, pay for travel, as with Expedia or buy a new car (e.g. the Audi R8 can be bought with BitCoins).

So now the BitCoin is involved in the circulation of goods. That alone is not going to bring the big splash, not yet!

Fiat money steps into a trap because of its debt policy (new money is created by debt, the so-called Giral mo-

161

ney) no one can deal with the debt and that means facing a collapse, the BitCoin comes and acts in the opposite way.

The BitCoin bases itself on credits and a value creation process for the generation of new BitCoins. However, since this process is only available for a limited time the last BitCoin will be made in 2140. Then there are exactly 21 million BitCoins.

Every four years, the output volume is halved, which raises the price to meet demand.

Basically, crises are the driving force for BitCoin. There, where previous trust is broken, BitCoin gives you a 'thank you' cost free! As currency.

Even if someone is only able to change 50 Euros a month, he or she will gain after one year through the REAL VALUE ADDED.

The real value, i.e. the actual value of the currency Bit-Coin, is therefore 1,700 US dollars.

Which factors are at the base of this knowledge?

- Amount of goods and services purchased in period X with BitCoins

- World currency depreciation

- Purchasing power and places of acceptance

- Confidence in security and privacy at BitCoin

162

- The 100 percent certainty that nobody can steal the BitCoin or crack the network.

- The certainty that no government, bank, people etc. can switch the BitCoin off.

- The digital scenes key currency

- Symbol for freedom of the people, due to 'not manipul ability' Smart Contracts

- Escape the totalitarian surveillance and digital enslavement

- Self-determination and self-responsible action

- Transparency and efficiency

- No trust in third parties, no trust in people "who provi de the BitCoin system, since BitCoin is not provided by anyone except computers"

- The end of the inflated administrative apparatus

- Insurance against unforeseen, pensions and others

- Simplicity in handling and obtaining bit coins

- Emergency response. If the state prohibits everything, BitCoins, just like cash, can be purchased on the street without online access.

- All other coins that exist, or are yet to come, are depending on BitCoin.

- BitCoin can be scaled up as required by SegWit and sidechains.
- Future-proof, always "up to date" and trend setting, in novative, these are BitCoin properties. We can do ever ything today, and no 'Old Coin' can offer that diversity.

THE BITCOIN IS THE ONLY DIGITAL CURRENCY WHICH IS NOT FOCUSED ON PROFIT AND THUS THE ONLY TRUE, HONEST DIGITAL CURRENCY!

To understand this, here's a definition of 'AltCoins' and Scam (MLM Coins):

'AltCoins'

Not intended as a means of payment. Used only as a proof of value for internal processes. Example Ethereum is not a „paid" coin, it is intended to reduce processes and save costs. Example energy sector or housing industry. By bypassing third party auditing, banks and financial service providers, governments worldwide can save millions, but must provide proof of value.

Every 'AltCoin' will have a similar function, but only very few will be of interest to the financial sector at all.

Almost 90 percent of all 'AltCoins' used use the argument that their technology is faster than the BitCoin Blockchain.

This argument no longer exists thanks to SegWit. Resulting in the 'AltCoins' losing value.

'AltCoins' live off their community. The generation of Alt-

Coins is lucrative only outside the target applications by mining. The difficulty level is currently still low, in the ratio expense / generation / income and exchange rate to BitCoins.

The demand is generated by Ethereum etc. due to the needs of the FinTec industry.

However, limited. 90 percent comes from the trading and mining of AltCoins and so the value at 100 percent is more speculative.

The BitCoin must always remain the number one coin, as it is a confidence indicator. Through its indispensable real value function, it reflects the trust of the population and thus also the trust in the 'AltCoins' and the digital economy in general.

This factor is neglected.

Another factor why AltCoins cannot overtake BitCoin, is the fact, that AltCoins would not have the right to exist without BitCoin. You are always forced to explain AltCoins via BitCoin. It is as if Samsung would always have to first explain the iPhone, before Samsung can even sell a smart phone.

And indeed, Samsung always has to face a performance comparison with the iPhone because it is not the smart phones origin.

SCAM COINS:

You will notice when a coin is non-existent when it is sold

through multi-level marketing. For certain there are some coins that are listed on Coinmarket Cap and are also dealt with by Github and Reddix, but the 0 value coins are in the starting blocks. Nobody buys a good-performing coin from someone (meaning nobody will sell their system to someone else who wants to put it on the market if the product is going well) because this person would not provide it.

So 99 percent of all coins and tokens are simply invented. The hype and the thought "I could miss the next Big Thing" is so firmly anchored in the mind that you buy everything possible, the main thing Blockchain, Coin or ICO and tokens are on it.

Scam coins and tokens consist from the simple belief and irrevocable fact that 75 percent of the world's population is unable to verify if the wallet and the mining are real. It could simply be a programming routine, an assembler program, which produces an output. Dazzle and deceive is the motto.

In order to be able to distinguish between authenticity and scams, you do not need much. Announcements for new coins, investments, and tokens typically look like the high-end projects from the magazines we buy, promising us a new and free life with machine-generated currency and we'll never have to work again.

While real 'AltCoins' are only for a specific user group and for certain applications, scam coins and tokens claim to have invented the "one-of-a-kind Blockchain that is super fast and 1000 times more secure than anything else."

166

The question of what the coin can do more than the Bit-Coin remains unanswered, because issues in speed problems have been solved.
SCAM ICO and SCAM CROWD FUNDING:

Here money is collected and misappropriated or simply something happens that the system never starts up.

The FinTec industry likes to use bogus arguments to even benefit from any progress, so-called hackathons are advertised, where freaks sell their knowledge for 5 minutes of fame and 10,000 Euros in prize money to a digital enslavement industry.

On the other hand, companies and book authors boast writing about BitCoins and then turn away from it.

Jack Tatar writes about BitCoins, take the status and money and plead for the FinTec industry. The values he spoke of in the book, were, "a necessary evil."

Aaron König writes about the benefits of BitCoin, which ends in the "Wiener Schule". Governing without government. State Coins, Europe Coins, etc. as DAO on a Blockchain.

Decentralization in the dictatorial Realm!

Sponsored and realised by Avalon Life, who fund their musings and castles in the air with tricks from the elementary school magic box: "become financially independent, follow the vision, do some environmental protection (emission), etc. 3 people and a multilingual first level support want to lead one million people into the light."

Yeah, sure!

Money is madly collected like water in a bottomless barrel.
THE BITCOIN REMAINS, BECAUSE ALL OTHERS MUST GO.

Such stories will soon go like the 'AltCoins'. In four years, the world will look different. We are heading for (and I hope to experience it) the next world economic crisis.

As early as 2019, this could be the opening door or 2020. Then the BitCoin value will experience an increase that we cannot imagine. The devaluation of the euro due to the crisis and the then-tightening regulations to prevent "bank flight" will accelerate the chaos, just as if you put oil into the fire.

By 2020, the output volume of the BitCoins will be halved, pushing the increased demand even further, pushing the real value of BitCoins to unprecedented heights. Therefore, a price for a BitCoin at its lowest limit is... $ 50,000.

The 'AltCoins' are increasingly suffering from a 'difficulty rise' and by the amount of Coins no others will make it to the top or create any value. Ethereum has learned what it means when you suddenly become so big yourself that you cannot keep up with the pace and become uninteresting for speculators due to the increase in difficulties. Then the course falls to 10 cents. Not to forget that 'Alt-Coins' are hackable.

Mining 'AltCoin' in 4 years will not be cost effective. Because there is no real worth in the coins the user community must grow and increase the trading volume and win fresh "buyers", so are the rules of the economy.

168

To make matters worse, the BitCoin will break the magic limit of $ 5,000. The resulting market capitalization brings the big "fish" on board. Infrastructure measures of gigantic proportions will be experienced as hedge funds, large investors and venture capital firms try to cover the risk by raising the REAL VALUE, creating more acceptance points, getting into the BitCoin world by forcing handling through a better haptic of the software.

Just one example: While the FinTec industry burned $ 45 billion in one year in developments that had to be phased out, Vooledger, RSK etc. had BitCoin with $ 1.5 billion in investment capital more achieved than anything else.

We see projects that bring the Internet into the BitCoin Blockchain, we can see how the protection of users from arbitrariness increases by obfuscation. All this gives Bit-Coin a confidence boost and a guarantee for investors that the money is safe. Because in contrast to the AltCoins and ScamCoins BitCoin cannot be regulated.

Everything has to run through a nerve-wracking consensus program, to bring changes about.

Features, that other coins do not have and because of marginal worth in relation to BitCoin, leads them to a stop, in this case.

AltCoin fans are not interested in the story behind it (Scam systems have brought many people to BitCoins, showing that you cannot do more with performance, but with a perfect blend of performance).

AltCoin fans are interested in two things: Difficulty and degree of volatility in order to gain profits through arbitrage, which then bring valuable BitCoins, since BitCoin Mining is only interesting with an investment of 2.5 million. Not really an incentive for home uses.

If the lever difficulty / price difference AltCoin - BitCoin is no longer correct, people will switch to BitCoin. And the value of the BitCoin will increase many times over.

This fact has been recognized by many, which is why not only normal systems now invest in AltCoin Mining, but also the scams - NVidea and Radeon have difficulties delivering graphics cards that operate AltCoin Mining.

This will inevitably speed up the difficulty of the coins and ensure that in four years, even the mining of coins is no longer profitable. Even with a low difficulty you would have to invest much more in hardware because of the price difference, which also means energy costs will soar in small areas as well.

The best for last

Anyone who buys BitCoins now and again is it through small amounts every month (50 - 100 Euros) will be able to save up a small fortune.

It is never too late. Only a question of proportionality.

Whether $ 2,000 is now 1 BTC or 0.5 BTC does not matter. $ 2,000 is and will remain $ 2,000.

The Euro currency or even a Fiat currency will be with us

for a few more years, whether we like it or not.

Roller coasters, headaches and abdominal pain in the world of the incomprehensible and the ignorant people.

"Oh the BitCoin is too expensive, because the transaction costs are too high!"

"The BitCoin will never become an accepted currency because of its volatility!"

"I never imagined that BitCoin, where I hold 40% of my investment account, then I'm here to make money and not to be Mr Right!" In 2018, still so little money transfer and remittance business is being used. This is a really miserable performance. Reason: this is a pure speculation object! Its volatility prevents its use in the B2B area. The holder is not willing to relinquish; the taker wants to hedge it immediately to get back to the FIAT world. No business has a price index in BTC. Worldwide, you know that a small bottle of Coke costs 1.5-3 USD more or less. Will we even experience this day? (Author: on which the BitCoin price is written on a blackboard)? Quote from a valued colleague of Cristiano Z.

2018 what happened? What are these statements? Am I dreaming a dream that will never come true? Do millions of people actually believe that a few fluctuations are so bad? The answer is yes! And why? They do not understand the financial world and that's why I will take a journey. A journey into the world of money. Its beginnings and its progress. Into a world of supposed stability and security from an old monetary system, which today serves only a purpose of measuring my wealth.

It came at the time as a pack of evolved humans who lived in a clan became aware that with continued growth, one man's labour force was no longer sufficient to hunt to the extent that there was a one-to-one exchange against a bamboo hut or plants that women had collected. Or simply, he didn't want to spend more hours hunting. Most of the time the hunters were on the road for days in large clans.

But the human mind would not be the same if we did not evolve in different directions. And so it is logical that at some point a decision came that only an exchange of goods was no incentive to continue. Considering that clan leaders mostly left their wives when the son was 6 years old and the average life expectancy was around 20 years. The 6-year-old was considered an adult and had to take over the tasks. Life in a nutshell. Keep it simple!

The need was born to create a value as an appreciation for hard work. An award, recognition, and a value with which the recipient could then rest for a while and still participate in the daily exchanges.

The people from early primitive population and those native populations we have studied hiding in the rainforests today that have not been sold out by civilization have something in common with us. They made a higher quality object of exchange from valuable mineral resources, from wood and other material.

That meant: One works for A PRIVILEGE/REWARD, TO GET MORE FOR HIS PERFORMANCE.
Upgrading performance is an stimulus. But why should

the owner of this privilege, now give up his "Urcoin"? He could still keep him and frame him to present this "award" to his successors as a pride of the clan and after 400 years, it would be worth more gold, because it would be an archaeological sensation, when it is found.

Quite simply: The human species recognised that other people felt stimulated to get this privilege and that the highest recognition was achieved in that the one who got it first through a "UrCoin" then handed it over.

What happened? People brought in more work and more new ideas. They teamed up in the daily harsh world to invent traps that made hunting easier. And the invention of "traps" was rewarded. Women cooked new dishes, found out what you should not eat. Quite simple, because they observed when somebody died, and what the cause was.

Services to the clan were rewarded. The pack system made the human a social being. At some point inevitably two different groups of communities met each other and these possessed different goods or one wanted to impress the women of the other group.

Then as a privilege an exceptionally high quality means of payment. And so it came that the already existing coins came into circulation. Obviously at some point it was no longer sufficient and had to be copied. Each copy, however, was a step in the direction that, as a privilege, it became less of a mass phenomenon, creating the first "inflation."

Thus, people were looking for higher-quality goods. And so it came about that the work of mining gold from a mountain was considered the highest privilege. Just like mining diamonds, platinum and silver today.

Today one still finds old objects of exchange from the past or mussel currencies etc.

The necessity of a bank? At first, banks were nothing more than value stores managed by someone who guaranteed that their precious privileges would be safe. So like a kind of artefact collection in a safe place with no museum function.

Robbery, envy, jealousy and lack of assets, hunger, etc, that was already well known by our great-great-great ancestors.

Through the introduction of the papyrus and final perfection achieved by Guttenberg's printing, we were in the position to show papers as proof of value in the form of a document, which we later used as an acknowledgment, including signature instead of a seal.

Thus, on the British note and the American note, an assurance of value was written on it. So our Fiat money today is a certificate.

But unfortunately, through the administrator's greed, our money was overvalued, thus giving out more paper to people than the gold or artefacts collection could secure in the bank.

Because nobody came to ask what its value was worth, but only recognising the pieces of paper given, the dissociation of money began. The debt, i.e. the reprinting of evidence, was without bounds.

And so that not everybody could print and reprint money, the dispensing of money was of course connected to the stock. More specific it was connected to difficult to get rare goods such as gold. Who does not remember the story that in the 1970s, the dollar's holdings were brought into safety in Fort Knox, where all the gold was stored.

But if something is scarce and ultimately gains in value through scarcity, but still is not able to supply the world population, then these 'goods' are only as much value as the faith still attached to it and that is not very much today.

Governments can devalue the belief and thus lower the price.

There has never been such a decline in the value of gold as there is today. We have seen India giving new paper undertakings overnight, abandoning the old promises, and nonetheless not having enough economic output to engage its people having a lower prosperity. So everyone is just out there for themselves.

Then the gold was collected in households, which should be a security for people in the future, even without paper pledges.

But gold is hard to divide and now that it's gone and India, as the largest importer of gold, stopped imports. The price of gold was driven down. In war, gold is not recognised in the country itself, and if you try to get the gold abroad at such times, there is someone who will take away your jewellery and your gold in the confusion and / or shoot you for it. It's so easy to devaluate gold.

Volatility

And there it is the legendary volatility. Do you remember the oil crisis around 1978? Sunday driving bans, etc. The oil shows us what volatility looks like. OPEC conferences to increase the flow rate or scarcity etc, meaning the worth of your papers jumping up and down, so the promise of privileges in paper form is broken every day by inflation. Worthlessness printed on a pretence and fostering faith through politics in a world where the words of politicians nobody believes anymore, but also has no other solutions and therefore the "continue to do so" that is the doctrine of our time. We devalue words and truths with lies and history changes on Facebook, Instagram, Snapshot, Google+, etc.

So words become volatile and also jump up and down for the ones who believe in their value. When I make a big group believe something that is not true, that group determines over the smaller group that tries to portray the truth.

But truth is a perspective. And because we all live in perspectives, money and the value of money is also a perspective and thus it fluctuates, so it is volatile.

What we see in Argentina, Zimbabwe, Venezuela, etc. Italy in the 80s. It took millions of promises printed on paper to even buy a meal...

The BitCoin

The BitCoin is a privilege. Yes, it is a promise that the BitCoin users will not be devalued. A huge difference. Bit-Coins are only available in limited quantities. Logically, the price of BitCoins must increase because the output is limited and in its total number is subject to a physical ending and is therefore not replicable.

As we have seen in the past, there has been more and more money reprinted to perfection, and thus money in circulation has nowhere the fundamental value that was given 20 years ago worldwide. The BitCoin is a promise for:

- truth

- stability

- justice

- added value

- compensation

- riddance of worthless promises

- drive for business

- combating poverty

- return of use to the hands of the community and not to some individuals

- prevention of abuse of power

This promise is not made by people susceptible to corruption. Not a victim of greed, envy and hatred for those who own more.

The BitCoin is protected by computers that are incorruptible!

Promises cannot be broken, the computer can not be bribed or tricked because mathematics is the basic truth of logic. No feelings can replace this truth. Phrases like "I know the inventor of the system personally" have not saved anyone from the disappointment by people, who have ultimately lost their money and find their unfulfilled trust in a pile of frustration, hatred and existential fears.

How many people do I know who say "I'm the best friend of..." and then, when you look at them, you realise that the one who said that is not on the same level as the other. Best friends, life buddies and then you leave your friend behind in poverty, the one who made you rich?

And who then seeks your approval because he has always sought that in life and cannot let go?

You see recognition, and if it's a written paper approval, it's only as valuable as the value behind it. And the acceptance of a one million in paper is very high in the Western world but nothing in the third world.

178

So the third world shows us that the volatility of BitCoin is just an illusion. It is not the BitCoin that dances up and down, but the price of the BitCoin, which shows its weakness. Its true face. Its statement "basically, I am worthless to systems that generate wealth through scarcity."

In Europe and the United States you do not need BitCoin and the banks do not need an ETH or Ripple here. By means of a deal, they could cut costs and also cancel the intermediaries in international payments. The USA is impressively demonstrating that this is possible by dictating prices to these middlemen, according to the motto: "If you don't play along, we'll kick you out as a money launderer!"

Pushing the world into digital money is a necessity, as are weaker species joining in a pack to defend outdated views. In the past, they killed each other in furious battles. The Middle Ages, with their tortures, crusades, and the bloodthurst, have shown us that people in the mass are mindless monkeys who run after a few elite monkeys, and somebody is going to come and disapprove Darwinians theory of evolution, when even members of parliament at the end of their words fight each other and a worthless paper, makes sure that people from all over the world, from a western point of view, for a lousy 100 USD, are being killed, children slaughtering their grandparents at home because of a "saving sock."

The BitCoin puts an end to disrespect and therefore it is not the BitCoin that is volatile but its environment through worthless promises, the Fiat money.

The ups and downs of the BitCoin is due to the inability of paper money to give its users a stable value, because only faith keeps it stable and the basis of our beliefs are that we have to have debts to create a new estimation of its worth and promising ourselves to pay it back in full. But unfortunately, in today's world, it is not possible to keep our promises because we are unable to take the money we need to settle our debts away from others. The labour we put into a company today has lost it's value through the wage-cost spiral, and the company's promise to look after you has been written off by the low-wage sector.

For example, a New York Uber driver has so many colleagues that today he has to work extra to feed his family. The value of the work and the result are no longer consistent and Uber simply cannot pay anymore.

And the economy says, "Well, you can make ends meet, but we are not there to balance your debts in the form of a higher salary."

"What does that show us?" We complain that the banks are taking away our money, at the same time the government should protect us from sharks and quote and unquote look after the protection of the consumer.

But what nobody fixes is our schizophrenic behaviour. We complain about highly speculative transactions that need to be resolved and on the other hand, we are the ones who want it.

The moment we sign a loan agreement with Media Markt for the new TV, the credit agreement for the house, we go into a highly speculative risk business.

180

While 8000 seemed to be manageable for the new TV (6 years of trembling, do I still have my job) the house is 30 (!) Years. In the golden times, that was in Germany, Austria and Switzerland 95 percent of the houses and values today are hereditary assets and the greed for inheritance tax is large, so that the heirs pay up again and have to take out loans on the house, mortgages.

And then it happens, the 4-headed family, where only the father works, because the children are too small, loses his contract. He has earned well as an independent service provider. The illusion to spread one's workforce ends when one comes, one who pays more and demands more and offers apparent safety that one no longer has to fight for new clients on a daily basis. At some point you have had enough.

Thus, one's own workforce becomes volatile and both contractors or employees and employers are at risk. The specialist decides to leave, and someone has to close his business.

And so the mountain of Fiat debt rises, which can no longer be covered by a promise of value or by offsetting the debt. And what must inevitably come then? Correct!

THE ECONOMIC CRISIS THAT FINALLY MAKES THE BITCOIN TO A GLOBAL CURRENCY

Many have foreseen crises that did not come and now I am going to go out on a limb and claim the economic crisis 2020 is coming. And yes, I can be wrong but that's still not going to change it, it's going to come anyway.

2008 was predicted a long time ago, in the year 2002. And everybody said: "See, it's not coming"!
I have just seen in the news the so-called "Government Shutdown" in the USA again. Like before, government officials standing in front of the authorities and not being able to work because the US had not paid the money into the pay office, as it simply was not possible.

And now they are back again. A non-regulated and ratified budget makes it possible and it is clear that the promise of a lifelong work is - Puff!- Up in smoke.

And yet people still going along with this.

The global economic crisis, which started from good old Europe, people will be driven into BitCoin to prevent the devaluation of money.

In Germany and Europe, people were incapacitated by a paragraph on the so-called "bank run" and lost the promise of their paper value, since the value in paper is electronic today. Cash is there, but you have to get it from the bank and if everybody wants to withdraw their assets from the bank, it is not possible because the bank has pledged the papers internally to other businesses. For example, like the Lehmann Brothers with its bad loans, which they have then sent off as high-quality to European banks, of which Deutsche Bank still sits on a time bomb, with the world's largest junk credits, alive only through government subsidy, but still paying high salaries.

And now the dangerous BitCoin, which shows that volatility in the price index comes from hollow promises in the Fiat world and investors using power as a means and not

182

as a trading object and sooner or later it will put an end to greedy people.

So the price is now bobbing around at 12000 (as of January 2018), because investors, after it had reached 20,000, saw that they had invested in bubbles, in futures exchanges and the call for ETF just, again and again, was rejected by the SEC, after the New York Stock Exchange had made a request.

And then disappointed investors got out. BitCoins are thrown back on the market and the price returns to its real value. Through the use of the BitCoin, like in Japan, the value increases. This real value must therefore reach a higher level, only then does On Top Trading make sense for infrastructure actions.

Instead, investors want to rush the technological advances that are good. The artificially created high fees, which consist only of the fact that the largest wallet operators, like Coinbase, Xapo, BitCoin.de and so on, take care, that untruths are circulated, such as "the BitCoin is too slow for the B2B business".

Those who understand the BitCoin as a privilege and have now built up a fortune through it, can actually sit back and wait.

I see it in my own business environment. It cannot grow enough for them because people are trapped in the old fiat world of dependencies.

Let them be. Whoever brings the BitCoin into circulation and buys it back to spend it, will appreciate the privilege, because with BitCoins you cannot go bankrupt, if you slow yourself down a bit.

Conclusion:

High transaction costs, volatility and speed are the illusion of an old world that is now digital and, like so many
things, time is changing and the howls of protest that we
have today will fade. SegWit, SegWit2x Coin, AltCoins,
all those promises from speculators and where are they
today? Some died before the show and all others are far
behind in the fairway of the BTC. No own value. If the BTC
drops they all drop. Or the community has no value. 1350
coins and many with 0 value or 1-2 dollars.

The BitCoin is lined up to unite them all in a world currency of increasing value, guaranteed until the Fiat world
is debt-free and thus the Fiat world being dissolved. And
then, but only when the last BitCoin comes out ending
the volatility and the BitCoin becomes a currency like the
good old fiat money.

In 2140.

People will replace the BitCoin, because only deflation can
create wealth equally. This assumes, however, that no one
can control the system, can neither change the ledger nor
intervene in the computer code of the Blockchain.

And that something like that could happen a second time,
nobody believes that. Because the trickery, scams and
central system show us that no one wants to give up are
own control again and ruining our faith in decentralized
promises.

184

The BitCoin is here to stay.

And saying the truth is difficult for everyone, especially if it hurts friends and acquaintances. To accept even more. Because truth is a matter of opinion or not?

Conclusion:

Included in the invention of the BitCoin was the search for the future, the hope for freedom and the opportunity to lead a simpler life, in which one gives all people the chance of value and participation in life.

We were united in the effort to achieve this goal. In the early years, we wanted to take the world by storm and make it fairer, easier and more transparent. And we wanted it disruptive. The old one out, the new pure one in.

There was no financial incentive to develop the BitCoin, just idealism and the fear of digital enslavement. Therefore we need Smart contracts to give us protection.

Today we see that the world of lies determines trading, that people's greed reaches its climax, and that those who want to live in the light, who believe in the energy of good, have a means of payment, a means of self-assurance, at times when hedging is a worthless term in a bubble of bankers, governments and speculators.

I have come to inform the world that the thought lives on and is being fulfilled, that every day victims are senselessly arrested from trying to escape from dictation, the martyrs ringing for a new world order, created by the people and the people whose name will eventually be hewn in stone after the BitCoin takes over.

If you do not wake up, you will live in isolation. Because with the need for BitCoins, will isolated the others and eventually force them to accept BTC, if they want to conclude business with the so-called "third world", which is then wealthy.

China used to be exploited, and today everyone is running to tem for business and taking big losses. And China dictates those and kicks them out, at will. See also the ICO debate.

The first ones who go through the door are being shot.

This is a call for cohesion. The BitCoin cannot disappear or be destroyed. And that counts for us as well.

And before we condemn the governments and our system, think about it, we wanted it that way, because we went to the polls and if not, we left the field to others. Do you want that too in the future? The digital enslavement?

To all those who look at it from the perspective of the old world:

Also your world in which we now live has arisen because you wanted to abolish older systems in order to realise your view of freedom at that time. And the achievements of this will not change through the BitCoin, but if one system of money has reached its end, a new one must come and if only a few have speeded up the end, money and control over the money belongs again to the individual.

186

Your shout at tax evaders and terrorists is only possible because the old system of Fiat money allowed it. Without BitCoins. But the system is at an end, because you must see that it is nothing more than evolution itself, not because of a few sinners.

And that is what I stand up for.

Jörg Molt Saturday, 20 January 2018

Glossary

An attack 51% theoretical possibility. By a takeover of 51% of the power (hash power) including all 1.6 million computers in the network, control over all computers and the entire Blockchain can be taken over and therefore "hacked".

Breeze Wallet is a special wallet that automatically creates access to the TumbleBit network, obfuscating transactions.

BIP (BitCoin Improvement Protocol) Describes the procedure for enabling, implementing, and enforcing new rules being set for the BitCoin Blockchain. Examples of BIP:

BIP 8 - Consensus, that only nodes are allowed to vote

BIP 9 - Consensus, that Nodes and Miners are allowed to vote

BIP 141 - Consensus, that SegWit is activated and also to double the space in blocks.

BIP 148 - Consensus, that SegWit is activated WIT HOUT double the space in blocks with the sub sequent Hard Fork

BIP 91 - Consensus, that SegWit is activated at 80 per cent approval (lock-in). Then the so-called BIT

188

1 must be set within 336 blocks (2 1/2 days) and the activation finished within 2016 blocks (Time of Difficulty adjustment about 11 - 14 days). SegWit 2x is based on GDP 141 and GDP 91.

BitCoin Unlimited Developers around the team of Roger Ver, who want to break new ground and see themselves as more innovative than the Dev Team.

Blockchain system for transferring and saving values in an Internet-like system. File sharing (file transfer program similar to Napster or Bit Torrent networks)

Cold Storage a) Possibility, to keep your private keys at home, for example as a paper wallet. b) At some exchanges you can store your keys on a server other than the Blockchain. Not safe, since the stock market can then steal keys.

Core Term for the "operating system" with which the Blockchain can be adapted. The core contains a wallet and the core is the gateway to the BitCoin world with this access. The core program is connected to a node or miner.

Dandelion (obfuscation of the IP addresses) With this technology it is possible including Tor connection, IP addresses to Blockchain system there and then back to the receiver to make unrecognisable. By hopping and flushing (redirecting the transaction to hundreds of other IP addresses), it is no longer possible to find the source of the transaction and there is no way to track a transaction based on the IP address.

Distributed Ledger s. Public Ledger, also called distributed database. Unlike the public ledger it is not visible to the public.

Double Spend BitCoins are files and like all files you can also copy and rename them, if you get there. You can now save the files on your machine and reset the Blockchain to an old state - similar to the system memory points when restoring Windows, after a blue screen error where windows was brought to a standstill before the error occurred, resets. If I bring my offline-stored coins back into the system, they are duplicated. Because the saving of the coins after the reset has not yet taken place.

Exchange Online currency exchange and fiat money exchange.

Fiat money all currencies that exist in paper form in the world and are not digital currencies.

Hard Fork No other term in the BitCoin scene has attracted as much attention lately as the dreaded Hard Fork. It is relatively simple. From Windows 8 you make Windows 10. The users decide whether they want to follow Windows 8 or Windows 10. In contrast to a Soft Fork a hard Fork is not compatible. This means that if any data is sent from Windows 8 to Windows 10 it will be rejected as invalid by Windows 10. A Hard Fork creates new AltCoins, so after a BitCoin Blockchain Hard Fork you can buy a new AltCoin if you want to. The BitCoin Blockchain and the BitCoin remain unaffected. On 01.08.2017 a new Alt-Coin was created by the SegWit 2x procedure: BC Cash. The Hard Fork triggered a split and that gave it the same amount of BC Cash as BitCoins had.

Hardware Storage (Cold Hardware Storage) Possibility to secure private keys on USB sticks, memory cards etc.

Hashpower Conversion of the computing power of a computer into rate power. The number of guessing attempts a computer can make to hash within a second.

Hash value Cryptographic key that cannot be calculated, but depending on the encryption depth and this is then expressed in a value.

Hidden Wallet Hidden Wallet is an alternative to the Breeze Wallets. Here is also an access to the TumbleBit network constructed.

Hot Wallet Private keys that are safely in the Blockchain and therefore cannot be stolen. Example: open bitwal.la account. Note the private key. The private key is not outsourced and thus cannot be viewed by bitwa.la. So he stores "HOT".

Lightning a side chain of the company that has also programmed SegWit. Lightning stores the transactions via SegWit and verifies them in its own network. If an error occurs, the transaction is aborted and sent through the normal Proof of Work procedure. Thanks to the SegWit connection, Lightning is safe because it does not verify the transactions, but only the digital signatures of a transaction, but they do not contain any values.

MAAS a side chain for smart contracts. Satohsi Nakamoto shut down the function of smart contracts prematurely in 2009 on the grounds that they were not safe. You can see at Ethereum that he was right. In 2010, Bithalo.org found a way to make it secure and set up a smart contract kit for marketplaces, decentralized job boards, and more. MAAS went one step further and outsourced the Smart Contracts. Then they were compressed according to a procedure (similar to the ZIP or RAW method from the computer world to make large files smaller). These contracts can now no longer be faked from the outside because the attacker must first decode them in the system of MAAS again. And since the system is integrated via SegWit, this is impossible.

Masternode In some decentralized structures, master nodes are extra generated. These are also often referred to as supernodes. Supernodes can perform various tasks outside the structure and act as sidechains, for example: In the case of the AltCoin, for example, they assume the function of obfuscating transfers.

Merkle Tree Binary system with which you can compare a maximum amount of different files with identical ones and thus detect damage or counterfeiting in very fast time and / or check logically related files to age. Basis for P2P networks.

Mimble Wimble Mimble Wimble originated from the French name for Lord Voldemort. Unlike TumbleBit, Mimble Wimble takes a different approach. The transactions are veiled by being pushed into each other. Thus, more than one transaction can be executed and later distributed to the recipients. Thus, transactions are like blind passengers and cannot be found.

Mining / Miner Name for a computer that runs the log and program of the Blockchain including the public ledger thus participating in the making and distribution of BitCoins, while ensuring the security of the network.

Node the receiver server, sender server and storage on the network at the same time and thus acts decentralized, since it no longer requires individual structures for servers. So-called fullnodes do not need tracers or central directories. They see the other nodes and are thus identical copies of the others. Since all have the same "level of knowledge", a manipulated computer would attract attention and be excluded from the net.

P2P network Peer-to-Peer network or often called People-to-People network. Represents the term for direct data exchange or value transfer without intermediary (e.g., central server, etc.). So, from computer to receiver, directly, without an intermediary server. So you do not need DropBox or something similar anymore.

Private Chains Private Chains are Blockchains that are not open to the public. So you can set up a Blockchain system for closed user groups. Example: Exonum - A private chain that is able to connect to the BitCoin Blockchain and thus provide users with the security of BitCon Blockchain.

Private Key This key is the pin and tan in the system. Those who lose this risk losing their money in the form of BitCoins.

Proof of Stake Process for generating new coins (PoS). The process is similar to a lottery where, for the purpose of the test, the participants determine how many coins will be put into the procedure for one month and a statistic on the majority of the participants will be drawn up. After the month, the coins will be released and by chance one of the participants will be rewarded with new coins. In this way, it can be ensured that no external attack has taken place. On the other hand, the PoS procedure is very vulnerable to Double Spend.

Proof of Work (PoW) A procedure for checking transactions stored in different blocks for accuracy and completeness, including through physical evidence in the form of heat generated by computational power (ie, workload).

Public Ledger Decentralized directory in which all transaction numbers, after completion of a review procedure, on a protocol and physical basis, are registered and publicly available.

Public / shared key public key. This key is the IBAN and BICC of the system.

Quantum Computer Quantum Computing - Latest computer technology (as of 2017), which is able to calculate more complex dimensions via the 3D model due to sheer incredible speed. For example, time can be calculated in several dimensions simultaneously. Example: A trains speed is 250 km / h. somebody is running on the roof and in the compartments. All three have different speed capabilities due to the laws of physics in the closed atmospheric space of the earth. The computer can now calculate complex issues, such as the creation of the universe etc.

Satoshi smallest unit of a BitCoins (eighth decimal place)

Satoshi Nakamoto Inventor Blockchain Algorithm and

BitCoin

Satoshi School World's First School of BitCoin and Bit-Coin Blockchain Technology.

SideChain Connection of another Blockchain to the Bit-Coin Blockchain, which can then perform tasks by outsourcing and restoring.

Smart contract digital contract that is self-executing and based on a logical if, and, then, or conditions. From the contract to the law, everything can be recorded and executed.

Soft Fork A soft fork is similar to the installation of Windows Office. After installation, Office must be enabled to restart the computer. For example, SegWit is activated via a soft fork. Unlike Hard Fork, Soft Fork is compatible with previous versions.

Swarm Elements of a file that has been split into several individual files and is "put together" again by the receiver. A swarm file is part of a whole file. These swarm parts may e.g. be monitored via a tracking server to ensure the integrity of the file from the receiver. The tracker can also assign identical parts of the same entire file from a different sender to specific recipients.

TumbleBit A side chain that allows the clouding of transactions. TumbleBit uses the so-called Tumbler method. Here several, equally high transactions are collected and mixed and sent out to the recipients. Thus, the receiver gets the transaction in the amount, but not with the same " serial number" that BitCoin had from the sender. A classification is therefore no longer possible. After all, the recipient does not care which country is on the back of a Euro coin. The main thing, it is worth 1 Euro.

Wallet the wallet and account in the Blockchain. Without a Wallet you cannot store BitCoins. The wallet is the access to Blockchain as part of this payment system.

About the author

Jörg Molt was born in Germany in 1972 and lives in Bavaria. At the age of 9, he had his first computer, a Commodore VC 20 and later on the C64, C128, Amiga 500, Amiga 1200 and Amiga 2000. Early on, he came into the 'scene' circles, learnt programming and hacking program codes.

Jörg Molt attended several computer conferences around the globe and was one of the first to use the early Internet. In 1993 he became aware of the so-called Cypher-punkära by old friends, with whom he grew up. One of the most flamboyant people of his time was certainly Kim Schmitz alias Dr. med. Kimble or Dr. Dotcom, with whom he had spent some time in his hometown youth centre, before Kim disappeared. In the mid-1990s, Jörg Molt then engaged himself with digital money systems and pursued this until the start of BitCoin. Therefore, he is one of the few people who have owned BitCoins from the very beginning.

Professionally and privately, Jörg Molt has continued his education in the IT sector and finally worked in various IT companies. Today he is in demand as a speaker at specialist conferences on BitCoin and BitCoin Blockchain, focusing on future development, security and decentralization.

In 2017, he was named in the Top 100 Trainer Excellence, by Speaker Excellence. Jörg Molt is one of the few experts for Blockchain and Crypto currencies: As a trainer, expert speaker and consultant, he is one of the most renowned specialists in Europe. Throughout many industries, he advises well-known companies and institutions worldwide on the implementation of digitization processes. As a solo miner and a member of the association at Antmine, he has helped to create significant structures. He built up capital and fixed assets in BitCoin from the start. Through the general development of Smart Contracts, based on the decentralised Blockchain, he founded an affiliate to mediate between users and manufacturers. Together with other experts, this resulted in the "Satoshi Competence School". In his easily understandable and humorous way, Jörg Molt enthuses his participants, and uses practical examples to show how the evolutionary technology is easy to apply.

www.ingramcontent.com/pod-product-compliance
Lightning Source LLC
Chambersburg PA
CBHW031059280326
41928CB00049B/1110